How to
FINANCE A HOME
IN THE
PACIFIC NORTHWEST

by
H. L. KIBBEY

Panoply Press, Incorporated

Lake Oswego, Oregon

| Cover design: | Bruce DeRoos |
| Cover & Title Page Art: | Krieg Barrie |

Copyright © 1991 by H.L. Kibbey
 Revised edition © 1993 by H. L. Kibbey

Printed in the United States of America

 Text has been printed on recycled paper.

Library of Congress Cataloging-in-Publication Data
Kibbey, H. L.
    How to finance a home in the Pacific Northwest : the complete guide to financing and refinancing a home in Oregon and Washington State / H. L. Kibbey. - - Rev. ed.
       p. cm.
    Includes index.
    ISBN 1-882877-02-0 : $15.95
       1. Mortgage loans- -Northwest, Pacific. 2. Mortgage loans--Northwest, Pacific - -Refinancing. 3. Housing- -Northwest, Pacific- -Finance. 4. House buying- -Northwest, Pacific. 5. Real estate business- -Northwest, Pacific. I. Title
HG2040.5.U6A194   1993
332.7'22'09795- -dc20   93-7690
                                                                                           CIP

Panoply Press, Inc.
P.O. Box 1885
Lake Oswego, OR 97035
(503) 697-7964

Publisher's catalog is available upon request.

ACKNOWLEDGMENTS

There are a great many industry professionals, friends, acquaintances and family members who have given me their assistance in the writing of both the original and the revised editions of this book. I thank them for their interest in this project and for their willingness to take time to help me research financing trends, double-check statistics, and proof pages. I am especially grateful for assistance from Tristania, Tohren and Byron Kibbey, Diane Gronholm, KiKi Canniff, Darlene Hess, Susan Weber, Matt Mallory, Julie Picard, Bruce Svela, Dave Kalinoski, Phil Gehring, Greg Haase, Tom Cusack, Dianna Hoelz, Mark Alspach, Carmen Wiswell, David Rogers, Dora Williamson, Phylis Somers, Sue Warren, Nanette Walkley, Bridie Halkoski, Jerry Ostendorff, Forrest Peck, Stephen Gordon, Fred Larson, Craig Tillotson, Kathy Eustrom, Kim Herman, Bob MacKenzie, Rhonda Rosenberg, Kurt Wittman, Bob Boyle, Duane Williamson, Ruth Klein, Ted Urton, Cheryl Eastman, Marlene Fromhold, Cliff Jones, John F. Scott, Ed Tyler, John Jeddeloh, Doug Bomarito, Cheryl Long, Harriet Smith, Judy Pearson, Bobbi Pearson, Colleen J. Watkins, Bruce Taylor, and Diane Mowry.

Thanks, too, to Bruce DeRoos, and Krieg Barrie, for turning their outstanding talents loose on the design and art for this book.

There are so many intricacies and complexities to the subject of real estate finance that it would be impossible to include all the minute facts, figures and conditions in one book. The information included in this volume, while carefully compiled, is not intended to be used as a substitute for competent professional or legal advice. When you buy, sell, finance or refinance a home, learn to rely on a team of professional advisors: your loan officer, real estate agent, attorney, and accountant to give you the help you need. Remember, too, that financing data is subject to change.

To Tristania, Tohren and Byron

TABLE OF CONTENTS

Part I

INTRODUCTION

1

Introduction

Financing a home's not easy. Even in the best of times, when interest rates are low and funds are readily available, choosing the perfect loan is neither straightforward nor effortless. Many borrowers start out with the best intentions. They assess their needs, plan their strategy, visit a loan officer or two and, in utter frustration, end up choosing financing by throwing darts or tossing a coin. Worse still, they may leave the choice to someone else—their loan officer, perhaps, or their father-in-law, who thinks 30-year fixed-rate loans are the only way to go.

How do I know this? Well, I'm the one they turn to when the doubts start creeping in. Over the years I've been asked plenty of questions, as a real estate writer and talk show host. Even at social gatherings, the talk inevitably turns to that perennially favorite topic of conversation: buying, selling or financing a home. The questions I'm asked are often quite fascinating. Generally I find that they fall into one or two categories. I like to classify them as either "Before the Fact" or "After the Disaster" questions.

Now the "Before the Fact" questions are ones I'm glad to be asked, questions such as: "Am I asking for trouble if I choose an adjustable-rate loan?" or "My mother-in-law is putting pressure on us to buy her home on contract; should we?" Good, solid questions— not spellbinding, perhaps, but generally interesting, educational, "meat and potatoes" material. It's encouraging to think that the callers may find a better loan or will be able to avoid a monumental real estate catastrophe simply because of the chance to understand the problem and the consequences before making a move.

On the other hand, the "After the Disaster" questions are the kind of material popular talk shows really thrive on. Sensational hard-luck stories or spectacular legal entanglements are fascinating to most listeners, who are no doubt immensely relieved to have managed to escape a similar fate themselves. Personally, I don't really *like* these questions because they reflect real suffering of either an economic or emotional nature, and often both. These are the questions that haunt me later, especially those with little prospect of a happy ending. After the disaster, there's often not much I or anyone else can do to make things turn out all right. That's why I wrote this book. I don't want to see homebuyers or sellers suffer great personal loss when so very many real estate disasters can be avoided simply by knowing the rules of the game, before you shake the dice and make the first move. Financing's no different from any other aspect of the transaction. If you know what to expect when you come face to face with a loan officer, you won't be intimidated by the dozens of loans you'll meet.

Finding the information you need to become an informed borrower is not always easy. Newspapers, magazines, radio and television all offer current financial news, but national coverage often fails to reflect the regional or local variations you'll encounter in your world. Then, too, it is often difficult to see the whole spectrum of real estate financing if your information comes to you in bits and pieces. This book will give it to you straight. All of the loans and other financing methods you're likely to encounter in the Pacific Northwest are here in these pages, along with my recommendations and suggestions for choosing the best and avoiding the worst.

2

How to Use This Book

This is a book for Northwesterners. It was designed to give homebuyers and sellers information about all the financing options available here in Oregon and Washington. Of course, much of the information is valid in any state. For example, there are conventional fixed-rate loans and FHA loans everywhere in the country. And people from coast to coast are buying or selling by means of land sales contracts. Certain basic principles remain the same wherever you go.

But beyond the basic similarities, there are some noticeable differences. Each state has its own unique set of real estate laws and practices; Oregon and Washington are no exception. You'll find that financing a home in either of the two is a very different matter from financing a home in Georgia, say, or Ohio, Montana, or any other state. Not only do interest rates differ and loan limits vary, but even the terminology changes from region to region. For example, 'land sales contracts' in the Northwest become 'land contracts' or 'contracts for deed' in other places. Types of loans that are popular in eastern states, for example, may be difficult to find here, or vice versa. Even federal government loan programs have local variations.

A FINANCING OVERVIEW

	Conventional Financing									Government Loans					Other Types of Financing				
	Fixed-rate 30-year loans	Fixed-rate 15-year loans	Biweekly Loans	Loans with Balloons	Adjustable-rate Mortgage Loans	Two-step Loans	Loans with Buydowns / Points	Graduated-payment Loans	Growing Equity Mortgage Loans (GEM's)	FHA loans *	VA loans *	FmHA Loans	State Housing Loans	Oregon DVA Loans	Seller-financing	Equity Loans and Other Seconds	Reverse Annuity Mortgages	Sweat equity	Farm Credit Services
Fixed interest rate	X	X	X	X				X	X	X	X	X	X		X	X	X		X
Adjustable or variable rate					X	X				X					X	X			X
Level payments	X	X	X	X						X	X	X	X		X	X	X		X
Varying payments			X		X	X	X	X	X	X	X	X			X	X	X		X
Early payoff		X	X	X					X						X	X			
Quick equity build-up		X	X						X										
Income restriction												X	X						
Sales price restrictions										X		X	X						X
Low-income subsidy												X							
Easier to qualify for					X	X	X	X	X	X	X	X	X	X	X				
Down payment under 5%										X	X	X	X						
No money down											X	X			X			X	
Refinancing	X	X	X	X	X	X	X			X	X						X		
Loans for veterans											X			X					
Loans for first-time buyers													X						
Buying a "fixer-upper"										X						X		X	
Farms/rural housing												X				X			X
Cash for equity																	X	X	

Pay particular attention to the loans marked "X". These specifically meet that requirement or are especially suited for that purpose although other types of financing may also be suitable.

* FHA and VA have a variety of loan programs to meet almost every need. Refer to those chapters for details.

In addition, Northwesterners are fortunate to have some wonderful loan programs that originate right in Oregon and Washington, such as the Single Family Mortgage

Program from the Oregon Housing Agency, and House Key, from the Washington State Housing Finance Commission.

As you read this book, you'll find some financing techniques that will be new to you; others will be familiar. Don't rush past one you have ruled out in the past: things change quickly in the world of finance and a loan program that failed to meet your needs last year may be perfect for you today.

This book gives you the information you will need to study the many financing possibilities and to compare them at a glance. How you use the book depends upon whether you are buying, refinancing or selling a home. However the chart in this chapter is a good place to start. It will help focus your attention on the types of loans that best fit your needs. It will also eliminate those loan programs that could not possibly work for you. As an example, if you earn $60,000 a year, you can immediately rule out both the FmHA and the Oregon Housing Agency programs, since they have income ceilings that are considerably lower.

As you look at the chart, you'll see various methods of financing (and refinancing) across the top. Down the left side is a list of needs, qualifications or requirements a borrower may have. Sellers, consider the needs of a typical buyer for your home. For example, if yours is a $300,000 home in perfect condition, neither "low income loans" nor "sweat equity" would apply. Buyers, if you're looking for particularly affordable loans, you can skip over the 15-year fixed loan, for instance.

Study each item on the list to see if it matches your situation. If it does, trace a path to the right to discover which loan programs would best solve that need, those marked "X". The chart gives you a broad overview of the loans and other financing techniques that follow. But don't limit your reading to those "most-likely-to succeed" chapters. Just as each type of financing has evolved from an earlier kind of loan, so the chapters of this book unfold. You'll find bits of pertinent information tucked into each one. A prospective borrower who has no interest in government financing, for example, may discover a previously unheard-of loan, one that could wrap up a home with easy terms.

Rules to Consider When Financing Your Home:

1. Choose the type of financing that is best suited to your income and financial requirements. Don't be swayed by financing fads. A loan that is right for the Joneses may be a poor choice for you.

2. Research government loan programs; in fact, research them *first*. They usually offer easier qualifying standards and lower down payment requirements.

3. Take time to comparison shop, first the types of loans that are available, then finally, the interest rates and specific market data. This book will make your job considerably easier.

4. Don't shop for interest rates alone. In fact, "What are your interest rates?" should be the *last* question you put to a lender, not the first.

5. Avoid the need to refinance later. If at all possible, choose financing you'll be happy with as long as you need it. Refinancing is expensive; refinance because you *want* to, not because you have to.

6. Don't choose a lender just because you've always had an account at that bank. In today's nation-wide loan market, that won't give you any advantages and may close your eyes to a better financing source.

Part II
CONVENTIONAL
FINANCING

Part II

CONVENTIONAL FINANCING

A conventional loan is one that is neither insured, guaranteed, nor funded by the government.

It's far easier to describe what conventional loans *are not* than to say exactly what they *are*. What comes to mind when we think of conventional financing are the non-government loans offered by banks, savings and loans (S&Ls), mortgage companies or mortgage brokers. These particular conventional loans are also known as *institutional loans*, since they're provided by a lending institution. However the range of conventional financing covers greater territory, since it also applies to financing from private sources, such as your parents or your credit union.

Conventional loans are transactions between you and the lender, without government funds or incentives. Because there's no direct government involvement, you'll find fewer limits and restrictions, but often less generous terms, especially in this post-S&L crisis era.

What Loans Were Like in the Good Old Days

If I had written this book before the late 1970s, my job would have been infinitely easier. Those were the "good old days", when choosing financing was a fairly simple procedure. Borrowers had far fewer decisions to make back then. If you wanted to finance a home, you had very little choice; what you'd end up with was a fixed-rate, long-term loan, with equal monthly payments over the life of the loan and wonderfully low interest rates that are just fond memories today. You wouldn't have needed a book like this, because there were few choices and very little confusion.

Then in the late '70s, the loan picture changed. Interest rates on home mortgage loans, which had fluctuated very little over the previous 30 to 40 years, now climbed to hitherto unscaled heights. For example, the interest rate on FHA loans first reached the double digits (10%) in April 1979. By September 1981, less than 2 1/2 years later, it soared to 17.5%!

You'd think the mortgage lenders would be thrilled with the prospect of higher rates, but on the contrary, they were just as dissatisfied about this turn of events as would-be borrowers were. The escalation had been so rapid that no one had time to adjust. Lenders still collected 6% interest on existing fixed-rate loans and were locked into that meager 6% return on their investment for the full 30-year term (or until the loan was repaid). At the same time, their cost to borrow funds was far higher. On the other hand, what homebuyer could afford to obtain-- or wanted to get-- new financing at 17.5%? The result was a stalemate, with the lenders anxious to make new loans but having to charge such high interest rates that the number of borrowers dwindled. Both sides suffered; the lenders were stuck with their old unprofitable loans, while a very large percentage of Americans could not afford to buy a home.

A Great New Crop of Hybrid Loans

Being amazingly resourceful, the lenders developed compromise plans. They experimented with new varieties of mortgage loans that would satisfy their investment needs, yet would be palatable and affordable enough to encourage borrowing. To do this, they took a look at three essential elements of any loan: the *interest rate* (which is the lender's return on the investment), the *term* (or scheduled lifespan of the loan), and the *payment amount*. They found that if they varied one of the three, they'd end up with a whole new loan. Within the space of a very few years, we saw a bumper crop of new financing ideas, such as shorter-term mortgages, graduated-rate mortgages, adjustable-rate mortgages, buy-downs, and balloons, plus an overwhelming number of variations and combinations of these. Even though interest rates have dropped since then, the innovations remained and others have been added to meet new financing needs.

But borrowers are understandably confused. Many homebuyers shy away from these innovations simply because they are different and a little more complex than the standard fixed-rate loans. Yet one of these new loans might be the best way—or in fact, the only way—for you to buy the home you've set your heart on. Don't rule out any possibility, however unappealing it may seem at first glance. Once you understand the personality of each of these different financing options, you'll be able to choose the ones that suit your particular needs. The loan programs we will investigate in this book are in their simplest form. Remember that each lender offers variations on the theme, so expect some differences as you talk to different loan officers.

Characteristics of Today's Loans

Home mortgage loans are *amortized loans*, which means that the loan payments (usually monthly payments) include a portion to partially repay the *principal* (the amount borrowed) and a portion to pay the interest that is due. The payments are calculated so that, at the end of the term, all of the principal has been repaid and all of the interest that was due has been paid. It's easy to figure the size of your monthly payments on an amortized loan; you'll find instructions as well as an *amortization chart* in Appendix I.

Interest on home mortgage loans is simple interest and, as such, is simple to calculate. If, for example, you owe $100,000 at 9% interest, just multiply $100,000 by .09 to discover that in a year's time (assuming you didn't pay back any of the principal), you'd have paid $9,000 in interest. Divide that by 12 to find out what you'd pay in the space of one month ($750).

What's particularly interesting about this is the portion of the amortized monthly payment that goes to pay the interest that's due. If we use the amortization chart to determine what the amortized monthly payment would be on this $100,000 loan, we find that it is $805, only $55 higher than the total amount of interest that is due. That means that out of the first month's payment, only $55 is applied to the principal; the remaining $750 pays the interest. (If you want to calculate the interest and principal for the second month, remember that the loan balance is now $99,945 and the interest would then be calculated using that loan amount.) As you can see, the principal on a thirty-year fixed-rate loan drops very slowly during the early years of the loan, gaining speed in the later years.

Understanding Loan-To-Value-Ratio

Before we study the individual types of loans, let's look at the term *loan-to-value ratio*, otherwise known as LTV or LVR. Since conventional lenders determine the amount of money they will loan you and the interest rate they will charge by your loan-to-value ratio, it's an important term to understand.

Very simply, your LTV is the amount of the loan, compared to the value of the property. It is expressed as a percentage. As an example, let's look at a $100,000 home and a buyer with a $20,000 down payment. First we calculate the loan amount needed:

Value of home	$100,000
Less down payment	-20,000
Amount of loan	$ 80,000

Then we can determine the loan-to-value ratio:

Amount of loan

$$LTV = \frac{\text{Amount of loan}}{\text{Value of property}} \times 100\%$$

$$= \frac{\$80,000}{\$100,000} \times 100\%$$

$$= 80\%$$

If that same buyer had only $10,000 for a down payment instead of $20,000, his LTV would be 90%. The larger the down payment, the lower the LTV.

Lenders prefer larger down payments, and hence, lower LTVs, because statistics show that a buyer who has more of his or her own money invested in the property will be less likely to default on the loan. In short, that means less risk to the lender. So the buyer with a low LTV can usually receive some concessions in return, such as little or no mortgage insurance and easier qualifying standards. This, of course, varies from loan to loan and from lender to lender.

The practice of offering such concessions could turn into an unmanageable situation without a set of guidelines. If borrower A (on the same $100,000 home) has a down payment of $19,000, while borrower B has only $16,400, just how much of a concession should the lender make? And what about borrower C with $13,000? How much higher should his mortgage insurance premium be?

Standarizing the LTVs

To simplify things, lending institutions have adopted a standard policy of grouping loans according to their LTVs. They have chosen certain LTVs-- most notably 95%, 90% and 80%-- and have eliminated those in between. Any LTV that falls between two of the categories is placed in the next higher one. Let's look at how this would affect borrowers A, B and C above, buying that $100,000 home:

	Down Payment	Loan Amount	Value of Home	Calculated LTV	LTV Loan Category
A	$19,000	$81,000	$100,000	81%	90%
B	$16,400	$85,600	$100,000	85.6%	90%
C	$13,000	$87,000	$100,000	87%	90%

According to our calculations, all three of these LTVs fall between the 80% and 90% categories. By applying the standard, a lender would consider all three to have a 90% LVR, regardless of the difference in down payment size.

Here's an important point to note. Borrower A is only $1,000 away from an 80% LTV. By increasing his down payment to $20,000, he may be able to save even more than $1,000 at closing or over the life of the loan. That depends upon the differences between his lender's 90% and 80% LTV loans and is something that should be discussed with a loan officer.

What about LTVs higher than 95%?

I can't name one lending institution currently offering conventional financing with a loan-to-value ratio greater than 95%, that is, a loan with a down payment less than 5% of the value of the home. (And in these post-S&L crisis days, even 95% LTV loans are becoming increasingly difficult to qualify for.) The risk to the lender is simply too great. On the other hand, government-backed loans, even those offered by these same institutions, are a different matter. There the government is willing to shoulder some of the risk through an insurance or guarantee program, and financing up to 100% LTV is possible to find. Any borrower with a down payment of less than 5% should study the section on government financing later in this book.

What determines the value?

Be aware that the value of a piece of property, in the eyes of a lender, is not necessarily the same figure as the agreed-upon sales price. After you apply for a loan, the loan officer will order a professional appraisal of the property and will use the results of that appraisal to determine the loan-to-value ratio. If the appraised value agrees with the sales price, all the LTV calculations you and the loan officer have been making will be correct. But if the appraisal comes in low, you may not be able to get as large a loan as you had planned.

We'll take borrowers A,B and C above as an example. The buyer and seller have agreed upon a sales price of $100,000, but let's say the appraiser estimated the home to be worth only $90,000. That figure, $90,000, is the one the lender will use to calculate the LTV, yet the seller still expects to receive $100,000 unless the deal is renegotiated. The chart below shows what a difference this makes in the the amount of the loan:

Appraised Value	Maximum 80% LTV Loan	Maximum 90% LTV Loan	Maximum 95% LTV Loan
$100,000	$80,000	$90,000	$95,000
$90,000	$72,000	$81,000	$85,500

With the appraised value of $90,000, borrower A barely squeezes into the 90% LTV category; it would now take an additional $9,000 down payment to obtain an 80% LTV loan. Borrowers B and C, asking for $85,600 and $87,000 loans respectively, now cannot borrow what they need, even with a 95% LTV loan. Both will have to come up with a larger down payment (although in B's case only $100) to obtain a loan.

The Down Payment Approach to LTVs

We have discussed how lenders focus on the amount of the loan as compared to the value of the property. But quite often borrowers like to think in terms of the size of the down payment, rather than the size of the loan. After all, that is cold, hard cash they have to come up with. So here is how to determine what your LTV category is, based upon your down payment.

First, calculate your down payment percentage, compared to the value of your home, using the following formula:

$$\text{Down payment \%} = \frac{\text{Down payment \$}}{\text{Value of home}} \times 100$$

For example, borrower A above, with a $19,000 down payment and a $100,000 home, has a 19% down payment. Now use the following chart to see what LTV loan category you would be in.

% of Down payment to Value of Property	LTV Loan Category
5% to 9.99%	95% LTV
10% to 19.99%	90% LTV
20% and over	80% LTV

Private Mortgage Insurance (PMI)

Private mortgage insurance, commonly known as PMI, is as popular among borrowers as the common cold and just as unavoidable for many. It is an insurance policy to protect the investor (lender) against loss suffered if the borrower should default and foreclosure becomes necessary. It does not protect the borrower in any way. PMI is required on most, if not all, conventional loans with an LTV ratio over 80%, and on many loans with an LTV of 80% or better.

The cost of the insurance is what makes borrowers groan, for they are the ones who foot the bill. The premium is based upon the type of loan (fixed-rate, adjustable-rate, etc.), the loan-to-value ratio and the degree of insurance protection required by the lender. Loans that carry a higher risk for the investor will cost more to insure, such as adjustable-rate loans or any non-level payment loans, especially those with deferred interest (a term that will be explained later.)

The mortgage insurance premium on conventional loans may be paid by one of three methods, depending upon the borrower's preference and the lender's requirements.

- The total amount may be paid in cash at closing. Estimate 2.25% to 3% of the loan amount as your one-time cost, although this varies widely depending upon the lender's requirements for this particular type of loan.

- The total amount may be financed, with the one-time mortgage insurance premium added directly to the loan amount. Not all lenders offer this option. An interesting point to consider: normally a mortgage insurance premium is not tax-deductible, but if you finance it, the interest you pay on your loan (including the premium amount) *may* be deducted on your IRS return. (Check with your accountant.)

- The first year's PMI premium may be paid at closing and each month thereafter, 1/12th of a year's premium will be paid in the regular monthly loan payment. Here are some sample costs for a $100,000 fixed-rate 30-year loan.

Sample Mortgage Insurance Costs				
LTV Ratio	1st year Premium	Paid at Clowing	Renewal Premium	Paid Monthly
90.01% to 95%	1%	$1,000	.50% per year	$41.67
85.01% to 90%	.50%	$500	.35% per year	$29.16
80.01% to 85%	.40%	$400	.35% per year	$29.16

You will note that the first year's premium is usually more expensive than that of the following year. From the second year on, the payment remains the same each month for the life of the loan, or in some policies, the premium is again reduced from the eleventh year on. Because the premium varies from loan to loan, depending upon the requirements of the loan investor, as well as the risk factor of the loan, it is impossible to give one cost formula that will apply to all situations. When you are ready to finance a home and know the size and type of loan you need, a loan officer can give you an accurate figure.

The only way to avoid mortgage insurance is to make a down payment of more than 20%, or to choose a type of non-conventional financing (a VA loan or a land sales contract, for instance) that does not require it. For information about FHA mortgage insurance, read the chapter on FHA loans, later in this book.

Now that the preliminary explanations are out of the way, let's take a look at the various kinds of conventional financing. The following chapters deal with those types of loans you'll encounter in today's market.

3

Fixed-Rate
30-Year Loans

A conventional, Fixed-Rate 30-year loan has an interest rate that does not vary over the life of the loan.* It has equal monthly payments that include both principal and interest, and is fully amortized.

I call this loan "Old Faithful" because it has been the most common home-financing method in the United States since its origin in the 1930s. Home buyers today use it as a yardstick to measure and evaluate all the other newfangled loan ideas. How does it compare? In many cases, "Old Faithful" does an excellent job of financing a home and most prospective borrowers start their loan search by giving it serious consideration. However, there are plenty of reasons why borrowers will want to (or find it necessary to) settle on an alternate type of financing. Let's look at some of the deciding factors, some of the strengths and weaknesses of the 30-year fixed-rate loan.

(* Loan documents often list specific circumstances under which the interest rate may increase. These might include sale, lease or transfer of interest in the property, or failure to meet the conditions of the loan agreement. These exceptions vary from loan to loan. Be sure to study all loan documents thoroughly.)

It Gets A+ for Stability

If you're looking for stability, predictability and dependability, if you can do without thrills and excitement in your financing life, then maybe this is the loan for you. From the day you sign the closing papers, you know exactly where you stand in the matter of monthly payments and interest rate. Thirty years later, you'll be mailing in your last payment and it will be identical to your first payment. A ho-hum life maybe, but a lot of us like it that way. The 30-year fixed-rate is by far the most popular loan in the U.S. today.

But it's Not Unbeatable

There are many loans that do better than Old Faithful at one particular feature or another. It may be that one of those will meet your needs better. So let's look at where the fixed-rate 30-year loan falls short. Affordability is a good place to start. Compared to some loans, such as the 15-year fixed, Old Faithful does very well. But other loans, such as the adjustable-rate or a balloon loan, are far more affordable. Here's why. Let's compare three 30-year loans, one at 6% interest (circa 1972), one at 10% interest and the third at 13% interest (all too common in the 80s). We'll use as an example a $100,000 home and a borrower with a $10,000 down payment who needs a $90,000 loan. Notice what a difference the interest rate makes in the borrower's monthly payments:

Interest Rate	Monthly Payment (Principal & Interest)
6%	$540
10%	$790
13%	$995

This is quite a hefty increase as rates climb, but what many prospective borrowers find even more astounding is the amount of income a borrower must earn to qualify for each of these fixed-rate loans. Since the income figure is based on the monthly payment, it's easy to see that an increase in the interest rate will mean an increase in income needed. Following the instructions for qualifying the borrower given in a later chapter, we find that:

Interest Rate	Income Needed to Qualify for $90,000 Loan *
6%	$2,700
10%	$3,400
13%	$4,000

* These figures are approximate, for a borrower with little or no other debt. Different homes and debt ratios could require a larger income in both cases.

In other words, in 1972, when rates were 6% a borrower needed to earn only $2,700 to obtain a fixed-rate loan. With 10% interest, that income must be about $700 higher, for the same type of loan. An interest rate of 13% pushes the income requirements to even greater heights. No wonder buyers look for alternate routes when interest rates rise!

As you can see, higher interest rates certainly narrow the field of possible borrowers. Since the interest rates lenders charge for their fixed-rate loans are higher than those for adjustable-rate loans, for example, a larger income is needed to qualify for a basic fixed-rate loan. Or, to look at it another way, a borrower will be able to qualify for a *larger* adjustable-rate loan. That is why "Old Faithful" may not be the right financing tool for you.

A Second Shortcoming: Interest

There's another reason borrowers choose an alternative method of financing and it has to do with the whopping amount of interest that is paid over the 30-year term. (Are you sitting down?) A homeowner with a $100,000 30-year fixed-rate loan at 10% interest will pay over $215,000 interest during the lifespan of the loan. Of course, the interest on most home mortgage loans is tax deductible, but even so, if I told you could reduce that amount by over $100,000, would you be interested? You can bet plenty of homeowners are, and you'll find ways to do just that in the chapters that follow.

Advantages of a Fixed-Rate 30-Year Loan

- Predictability: Your monthly payments (excluding taxes and insurance) will be exactly the same for the next thirty years. There will be no surprises, no unexpected increases or large balloon payments to plan for.

- Security: Your loan will not be affected in any way by changes in the economy.

Disadvantages of a Fixed-Rate 30-Year Loan

- Higher interest rate: There are loans with lower interest rates, at least initially, than this.

- Higher monthly payments: These loans have higher monthly payments (again, at least initially) than some other types of loans, such as the Adjustable-Rate Loans.)

- More difficult to qualify: Because the monthly payments are higher, a borrower must have a higher income to qualify for a 30-year fixed rate loan, as compared to some other types of loans, and

- Long-term commitment: This could be an advantage or disadvantage, depending upon how satisfied you are with your interest rate. If rates decline, you may wish you had chosen an adjustable.

4

Fixed-Rate
15-Year Loans

A Fixed-Rate 15-Year Loan is similar to a fixed-rate 30-year loan, but with a shorter term, resulting in a faster accumulation of equity and less interest paid over the term of the loan.

If you are fortunate enough to have a higher income than necessary to qualify for a fixed-rate 30-year loan and the ability to make larger monthly payments, this may be just the loan for you!

The Good News...

But who wants higher monthly payments? According to loan officers, a surprising number of borrowers choose this method of financing. Here's why: for starters, they can save 15 years' worth of interest by paying off a loan in 15 years instead of 30. Second, lenders usually offer a lower interest rate on their 15-year loans (1/4 to 1/2 of 1%), thereby increasing the savings.

And the Bad . . .

Of course, there are disadvantages too. Because the loan must be repaid in 15 years, the amortized monthly payments are higher. This, in turn, means that a higher income is needed to qualify for the loan.

Quick Build-up of Equity

Another factor to consider is the speed at which the owner's equity is built up. Since the extra amount paid each month is applied to the principal, the loan balance is reduced much faster than for the 30-year loan. This sounds like an unquestionable advantage, having a home completely paid for in 15 years. However, it could also be a disadvantage if the home is sold. This is especially significant if the loan is assumable. The greater the owner's equity, the greater the difference between the loan balance and the new sales price. The new buyer assumes the loan but must somehow pay the seller that difference. Most buyers find it easier to assume a larger loan with lower monthly payments and a smaller equity to cash out. In difficult markets, owners may have trouble getting all of their cash back out of the home.

Comparing 15-year and 30-year Fixed-Rate Loans

Here's a comparison between three $100,000 fixed-rate loans, a 30-year loan at 10% interest, and two 15-year loans, one at 10% interest to illustrate the effect of the shorter term, and the other at 9.75% to show the additional interest savings at a lower rate.

You may be surprised to learn that the monthly payments for the 15-year loan are not twice the size of the 30-year loan payments. In fact, they're usually only about 14% to 19% higher. That reflects the savings in interest over the life of the 15-year loan.

Term	Loan Amount	Interest Rate	Monthly Payment (P&I)	Interest Paid 1st Month	Principal Paid 1st Month	Balance After 1 Month	Total Interest Over Term	Income Needed to Qualify*
30-yr	$100,000	10%	$878	$833	$44	$99,956	$215,926	$3,133
15-yr	$100,000	10%	$1075	$833	$241	$99,759	$93,429	$3,681
15-yr	$100,000	9.75%	$1059	$813	$247	$99,753	$90,685	$3,636

* *Income figures are approximate for a borrower with no debts, paying $250 per month property taxes and insurance.*

As you can see, if the interest rate and the loan balance are the same, then the same amount of interest will be due, regardless of the term of the loan. Anything over and above that interest amount will be applied to the principal, thereby lowering the loan balance. You'll notice from the chart that after one payment, the principal on the 15-year loans has been reduced by approximately $200 more than that on the 30-year. That's just the first month! Since the loan balance on the 15-year is now lower than the 30-year, the second month will bring a savings in interest, too. (Interest due each month is based on the loan balance; a lower balance will mean a lower amount charged to interest.)

Combining the Best of Both

If your lender will allow it, you may borrow some of the techniques and advantages of the 15-year loan to use with your existing 30-year loan. By voluntarily increasing your monthly payment each month, you can reap the interest-saving benefits and at the same time lower your loan balance at a much faster rate. On the other hand, you are not locked into the higher payments and can drop back to the regular amount at any time. This "safety net" could come in handy if you run into financial difficulties. A word of warning: Be sure to ask your lender's permission to do this. Some loan documents include a penalty for payments beyond the call of duty. That would take the fun and profit out of this technique in a hurry.

Advantages of a Fixed-Rate 15-Year Loan

- Dramatic savings in interest (compared to 30-year loan).

- Usually available at a slightly lower interest rate.

- Rapid build-up of equity (although this could also be a disadvantage.)

Disadvantages of a Fixed-Rate 15-Year Loan

- Higher monthly payments.

- Higher income needed to qualify for the loan.

- Rapid equity buildup means more of your money locked up in an asset that's certainly not liquid.

LoanLingo: Equity

The equity you have in your home is that portion of the home's value that is over and above the amount financed. If you buy a home with a $10,000 down payment, you have $10,000 equity the day you sign the closing papers.

There are 3 ways to change your amount of equity—one passive, two active:

1. Wait 'til real estate market prices change. When your home's value increases with neighborhood trends, your equity will increase.

2. Change your financing. Paying down a loan will increase equity; adding extra financing will lower it.

3. Change the condition of your home. Remodeling may increase the value and increase your equity at the same time.

5

Biweekly Loans

A Biweekly Payment Loan has a two-week (rather than monthly) payment schedule, requiring the borrower to make 26 payments per year, each equal to one-half of a standard monthly payment.

Could you be talked into making a half-payment every two weeks instead of twelve full-size monthly payments? Most borrowers would say, "Sure, but why bother?" At first glance, it appears you'd be accomplishing the same goal either way, while wasting twice as much postage to mail your payments to the bank. But wait! Simple arithmetic shows that those 26 biweekly payments add up to the equivalent of 13 monthly payments in each year. That's one whole extra monthly payment that somehow got paid, quite painlessly. Since the same amount of interest is due, whether you make 12 or 13 full payments, the extra amount paid is pure gravy. It will be applied to the principal balance of the loan, reducing it more quickly than that on the standard loan. As the principal is lowered, even less interest will be due each subsequent month on the biweekly loan than on a regular 30-year plan. Consequently, the biweekly loan is repaid faster than its standard counterpart. If we compare two $100,000 fixed-rate loans at 10% interest, one a standard 30-year loan with monthly payments, the other a biweekly loan with payments equal to one half the monthly payment of the first loan, we notice a visible difference in the decreasing loan balances. After two years, the standard loan has a balance of $98,818, while the biweekly balance is already down to $96,876 After five years, the gulf has widened: $96,541 on the standard loan, $90,850 on the biweekly. In just 21 years, the biweekly balance is down to zero, while $61,968 is owed on the standard loan, plus another 9 years of interest. Overall, the biweekly loan saves $76,282 in interest!

Pros and Cons of Biweekly Loans

Sound a little like the 15-year fixed-rate loan? There are distinct similarities. While the payment plans are different, both loans build equity faster than a standard 30-year loan by increasing the amount of the payments. The disadvantages are similar, too: their accelerated payments make them both more difficult to qualify for, and the rapid equity build-up on each can just as easily be considered a drawback. Real estate is certainly not a liquid asset and you may have difficulty liquidating that equity if you should need to obtain funds quickly.

The biweekly loan is offered by few lenders, primarily because the extra payments add to the processing costs. As a result, many lenders (and the secondary market investors who buy loans from lenders) insist that an automatic-payment checking or savings account be set up for biweekly loans, to pay the lender directly.

Advantages of a Biweekly Loan

- Accelerated payments offer interest savings.
- The payment schedule yields the equivalent of an extra monthly payment a year, painlessly.

Disadvantages of a Biweekly Loan

- More income needed to qualify.

6

Loans With Balloons

Loans with Balloons are due and payable in full on a specified date, commonly 5 or 7 years from the origination, before the end of the amortization period.

Who says it's difficult to clean up a tarnished reputation? These loans did and now they're a respected component of any lender's portfolio. Balloons aren't a new idea; they've often been used with seller financing. Until recently, though, the balloon loans that were offered by conventional home mortgage lenders were unnecessarily risky. There were no safety features to guard consumers who were foolish enough, or desperate enough, to stumble into them. That changed when Fannie Mae and Freddie Mac agreed to purchase a modified form of balloon loan. It's not suitable for every borrower, but at least much of the risk has been eliminated.

How a Balloon Loan is Structured

Loans with balloons must be paid off at a certain date specified in the loan documents. Today's balloon loans are usually fixed-rate loans that are due and payable after the first 5 or 7 years. If you want to learn the lingo, here's what insiders call them: Thirty-Due-In-Five or

Thirty-Due-In-Seven loans. Sometimes you'll hear them called Rollovers or Loans With Calls. No matter what the name, the essence is the same. The entire principal balance is due at the call date. Even if a sizeable chunk of your paycheck has been paying down the loan, you may be quite surprised to find that the balance is still very high, even after 5 years. Take a look at a sample $100,000 loan (30-year fixed-rate) at 10% interest.

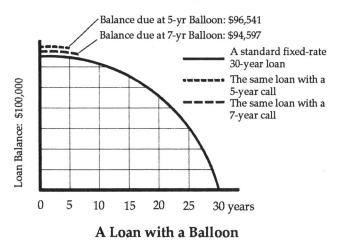

A Loan with a Balloon

After 5 years of faithfully making the required payments, the principal balance is still $96,574. After 7 years, there is still $94,649 owed. In a 30-year amortized loan the principal is reduced very slowly at first, as many borrowers found out when their loans became due and payable. For many, a balloon loan was a fast track to foreclosure.

Reducing the Risk

Today most of the balloon loans you will encounter come with a built-in escape hatch. If you meet the lender's conditions, the loan may be reset and extended beyond the due date for the remaining 23- or 25-year term. Here are sample conditions similar to those commonly found on this new breed of balloon loans. All of the conditions must be met in order to extend the loan:

- The borrower must still own and occupy the home.

- No other liens or encumbrances (equity loans, for instance) against the property may exist.

- The new reset note rate cannot be more than 5% above the original note rate.

- The borrowers must notify the lender in advance (the time is specified in the documents) that they wish to reset and extend the loan.

As in any type of financing, you'll find plenty of variations among balloon loans. Your lender may have different conditions for resetting and extending the loan. Some lenders (but mercifully few) offer balloon loans with no safeguards at all.

Most balloon loans start with an interest rate slightly below that on a 30-year fixed-rate loan (1/2 to 3/4 of 1% lower), but when the loan is reset, the interest rate will no doubt change (most of today's balloon loans will reset the rate to about 1/2 of 1% above the prevailing market rate for a 30-year fixed-rate loan). There's usually a processing fee charged (estimate $250 to $500), but at least the financing can continue, if necessary, without the need to re-qualify and refinance.

Lenders recommend balloon loans to borrowers who are fairly certain they'll be moving before the deadline. They're often considered "executive loans" since they're excellent for frequent transferees. But watch out for a slow real estate market. If you're transferred elsewhere and the home doesn't sell, you could end up forfeiting the extension and losing the home through foreclosure when the loan becomes due.

Advantages of a Loan with a Balloon

- Usually lenders offer a small reduction in interest rate (as compared to a fixed-rate 30-year loan).

- Because of the lower interest rate, they're slightly easier to qualify for.

Disadvantages of a Loan with a Balloon

- Even with the safeguards, there is some risk with a balloon loan.

- Certain other loans (1-year ARMs, for example) rank higher in "affordability".

LoanLingo: Mortgages

So often you'll hear people say, "I'm going to get a mortgage on my home." Sound OK? No, I'm afraid they've got it backwards. Borrowers give a mortgage to their lender, not get one. A mortgage is not a loan; it's a security document that offers your home as collateral for the loan. As such, it gives your lender the right to claim the amount of the loan balance (plus legal fees) if you should default. To make matters even more confusing, lenders today in the Pacific Northwest rarely use mortgages; trust deeds have taken their place as the most popular form of security device.

7

Adjustable-Rate Mortgage Loans

An Adjustable-Rate Mortgage (ARM) Loan has an interest rate that fluctuates according to a specified index. The rate is adjusted, and corresponding changes are made in the monthly payments, at prearranged intervals over the life of the loan.

Just when home mortgage interest rates were approaching their record highs in the early '80s, along came Adjustable-Rate Mortgage Loans (Arms), with the hope that they would solve many of the problems that had troubled both lenders and homebuyers. Since the interest rate on an ARM was designed to "go with the flow," lenders would no longer be stuck holding unprofitable low-interest loans. Here was their chance to rewrite the rules for the no-win financing game we found ourselves forced to play.

Homebuyers needed help, too. With interest rates reaching frightening new heights each week, who could qualify for a loan large enough to buy a home? Not many Americans. And if few could buy, few could sell. Homeowners were forced to drop their asking prices to drastic new lows in order to to find a buyer who could afford the financing.

Adjustable-rate loans solve both problems. Because the lenders do not have to bear the entire loss in interest if rates rise, they can afford to be generous. Borrowers willing to share the risk by accepting an ARM, will be offered an interest rate that is significantly lower — at least at the outset — than that for a fixed-rate loan. The lower rate produces smaller initial monthly payments and these, in turn, usually make qualifying easier.

How An ARM Works

All adjustable-rate mortgages have four factors in common:

1. Period of Adjustment: This tells how frequently the interest rate will be adjusted. For example, with a 1-year ARM, the interest rate will be adjusted each year. The most common are the 6-month and 1-year ARM, with other varieties offered, such as the 3- and 5-year ARMs. For the gamblers in our midst, there is even a 1-month ARM!

2. Note Rate: This is the initial interest rate the lender will charge for the first period of adjustment. In general, the shorter the period of adjustment, the lower the note rate. (If it is more than 2% or 2.5% lower than the interest on a fixed-rate 30-year loan, be wary. This may, in fact, be a Graduated-Payment ARM, to be covered later in this chapter.)

3. Index: This is the guideline that is used as the basis for adjustment. If the index rate has increased at the time of adjustment, the interest rate on the ARM will be raised accordingly. Different indexes are used, the most common today in the Pacific Northwest is based on the index of U.S. Treasury Securities. (More about indexes later.)

4. Margin: This amount is added to the index rate to establish the interest rate on an ARM. For example, if the index on an ARM is the 1-year Treasury Index rate, and that happens to be 7.00% at the time of adjustment, the new interest rate would be 7.00% plus the margin. If the margin is 2.75%, the new rate would be 7.00% + 2.75% or 9.75%.

This chart shows how the interest rate on an ARM is adjusted. Notice that fluctuations in the index only affect the ARM's rate at the time of adjustment.

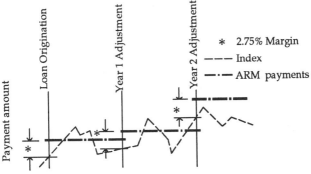

1-Year ARM with a 2.75% Margin

Safety Devices Mean Sharing the Risk

The first ARMs through the starting gate were uncontrolled beasts that made potential borrowers very nervous. What would happen if the index took a flying leap, suddenly landing 10 points higher? On some loans, the borrower was stuck with outrageously high payments and suffered from a near-fatal case of what is known as "payment shock." The lender sat back and counted the profits, or initiated foreclosure proceedings against the unfortunate gambler.

Today's ARMs are tame by comparison. Safety features have been added to protect the consumer and while the index still fluctuates, its effect on the new ARMs can be limited.

Here are some safety features to shop for in an ARM:

1. **Lifetime Cap**: This is the maximum percentage of interest increase or decrease that may occur during the term of the loan. For instance, a 5% lifetime cap on an 8.25% ARM means that the interest may never exceed 13.25% or drop lower than 3.25%.

2. **Adjustment Cap**: This is the maximum percentage of interest increase or decrease that may occur at the time of adjustment. On 1-year ARMs, it is often called the Annual Cap. A 8.25% ARM, for example, with a 2% adjustment cap may be increased to no more than 10.25% on its first adjustment. On each succeeding adjustment, an additional 2% may be added. Decreases work in the same way.

3. **Payment Cap**: This is an option that is available on some ARMs, but fortunately not many these days. Instead of regulating the increase in interest charged, a payment cap simply limits the increase in payment amount when the rate is adjusted. A first it may sound like a good idea, but take a closer look! For example, on an ARM with monthly payments of $700, a 7.5% payment cap would prevent the payment from exceeding $752.50 at the first adjustment, no matter how high the index has climbed. Yet if you are limiting the payment amount but not the interest rate, your payment may not be large enough to cover the interest that is due. What happens to all that unpaid interest? It's certainly not simply ignored; it's added to your principal loan balance where it costs you even more in the long run, as you pay interest on your (deferred) interest. This is what is known as "negative amortization". (Read more about it later in this chapter.)

Amortization Of An ARM

Most ARMs have a 30-year term. In other words, their initial payments are amortized over 30 years. Each time the interest rate on an ARM is adjusted, the payments are recalculated and re-amortized over the remaining term. For example, on a 3-year ARM, at the first adjustment there will be 27 years remaining. Therefore, to calculate the new payment amount with an amortization chart (Appendix I), use the new interest rate, the remaining loan balance, and a 27-year term.

Shopping For An ARM

It is not as easy to shop for an adjustable-rate loan as it is for a standard fixed-rate loan because there are so many variables to consider. Each lender may offer several ARMs with different adjustment periods, note rates, margins, indexes, and caps. In addition, there are some other features, such as convertibility and assumability, to investigate. You may find it easier to plot a hypothetical case for each loan. Which would suit your needs better? What would happen to each if the index rose? Your loan officer has followed the path of the ARMs and can help you understand the limits of risk or reward with each different loan.

Which Index Is Best?

The most common ARM indexes used today by Pacific Northwest lenders are the 1-Year Treasury Index (an average of U.S. Treasury securities adjusted to a constant maturity of one year), and variations thereof (such as the 3-year or 5-year Treasury Index for 3-and 5-year ARMs respectively). Yet it's possible to find loans based on a wide variety of indexes; one lender may offer a choice of loans with two or three different indexes . Choosing the "best" one is not easy. All of the indexes fluctuate, of course, in concert with the nation's overall economic picture, but they fluctuate at frustratingly different tempos.

To make matters even worse for the bewildered borrower, some indexes have names that don't exactly roll off the tip of one's tongue. Most of us have heard of the U.S. Treasury Securities Index. And then there's the Cost of Funds Index, not quite as widely used in the Pacific Northwest at the moment. Just recently, a few lenders began offering ARMs based on the weekly average for certain Certificates of Deposit (CDs). How would you like your loan officer to suggest this tongue-twister of an index? It's guaranteed to leave even stout-hearted borrowers gasping: the Federal Home Loan Mortgage Corporation posted yield requirement for 60-day delivery of fixed-rate 30-year loans plus 50 basis points index!

Just about any standard, readily verifiable rate could be used as an index. In fact, you'll find the current rates for a number of different indexes listed in the real estate or financial sections of major newspapers. If you're trying to evaluate an index, your loan officer should be able to provide you with a history of its meanderings. Once you have narrowed down your choice to loans based on different indexes, study a graph of each to see how its volatility would affect your interest rate. You'll find, for instance, that the Treasury Securities Index reacts very quickly to economic changes, with lots of sharp peaks on its graph, while the Cost of Funds Index reacts to events with a lag time of several months, showing gentler curves on its chart. If you're planning to choose a 6-month or 1-year ARM, you may be able to put this information to profitable use, by choosing an index that will react predictably to near-term economic trends you can foresee. But beyond the short-range planning, it's impossible to determine what the outcome of your rate will ultimately be. It's far more important to understand how your index moves, so that you can be prepared to make changes if necessary (converting or refinancing) at an opportune time.

Graduated Payment ARMs (GPARMs)

When you're ARM-shopping, watch out for interest rates that seem too good to be true. In many cases, they are! What you may have found is a ARM with an unusually low rate, a special introductory "teaser" rate on which the initial payments are based. Unfortunately, the actual "note rate" that will determine the interest you'll be charged is higher and the low initial payments are too low to cover all the interest that is due. By now, you know what happens to that unpaid interest; it's deferred, of course, and added to the original loan balance. No wonder it's called "negative amortization"! Your amortized loan isn't being paid off, it's getting bigger by the month. If you've ever tried to sell a home in a declining market, you can see the danger with deferred interest. Somewhere along the line, your increasing loan balance and your decreasing property value cross paths; you find that even if a buyer is willing to pay the full market value, you'll still owe the bank money out of your own pocket. These are great loans to avoid, but fortunately they're not widely promoted these days in the Northwest.

Convertibility To A Fixed Rate Loan

Even though an ARM loan makes good sense at the moment, there may come a time when you'd rather have a fixed-rate loan. It's possible to choose an ARM with a provision that allows the borrower to convert to a fixed-rate loan at a later date for little or no additional loan fees. This provision is not free; lenders often charge a slightly higher interest rate — usually one-eighth to one-quarter of one percent over the rate on a standard ARM. While this sounds like a handy feature to have, especially if interest rates decline, fewer than 10% of ARM borrowers actually exercise their conversion option. The reason is very simple: when they get ready to convert, they quite often discover that the fixed interest rate they'll be converting to is actually higher than that on many brand-new loans. It's calculated quite legally, using a standard formula, and may still be worth the conversion, but it's a good idea to investigate a conversion option thoroughly before paying extra for it.

You'll find that different loans have vastly different conversion policies. With some ARMs, conversion is possible only at specified times, for example, at the time of loan adjustment. Other ARMs permit conversion on any banking day, but only during the first few years. Be sure to ask about these details and inquire whether or not they are subject to change before your ARM is converted.

Buydowns With An ARM

Both permanent and temporary buydowns are available for adjustable-rate loans, although not every lender offers this option. Buydowns make ARMs even more affordable by reducing the monthly payments on a permanent or temporary basis. That, in turn, often makes it easier for the borrower to qualify for the loan. This offers the same result as the Graduated-Payment ARM but without the problem of deferred interest. Refer to the chapter on Loans With Buydowns to learn how to calculate the fee.

Assumability Of An ARM

Lenders are more likely to permit a buyer to assume an ARM than a fixed-rate 30-year loan. The reason is, of course, that the ARMs are more profitable for a lender since they keep pace with the economy. But that does not mean that all ARMs are assumable, and those that are usually have strings attached.

For example, it is not uncommon for the lender to retain the right to adjust the interest rate at the time of assumption, even if the next official adjustment date is years away. That may make the assumption less attractive than a new loan with a buydown. As in other assumptions, the new buyer will usually be required to qualify for the loan, based upon the new rate and payments. Keep in mind that prospective buyers who are searching for the perfect assumption would much prefer to assume a fixed-rate loan. So while the assumability feature on an ARM could, perhaps, be put to good use, it should never be the primary reason to choose an ARM over other non-assumable financing.

Case History: Marisa James

Marisa certainly didn't need an "affordable" loan. She could qualify for just about any loan she felt like pursuing. So when I suggested that an ARM would be perfect for her, I could tell that she was sure I had failed to recognize the golden aura surrounding her financial statement. She was clearly offended, but stayed long enough to listen to my reasons.

Marisa owned a home in Oregon, free and clear, but was accepting a promotion that would transfer her to Seattle. She had her home on the market and had already found a home she wanted to buy but was having great difficulty choosing the perfect loan. She was concerned because she was due to retire in three years and simply didn't want a mortgage loan hanging around much after that, like an unwanted guest. She liked her homes free and clear, without any debt. So just as soon as her home in Oregon sold and she received a couple of substantial bonus checks that were coming her way, she'd be paying off that mortgage and enjoying the debt-free life once again.

The question was put to me: should Marisa choose a 30-year fixed-rate loan or a 15-year fixed? Neither seemed to make good sense. Instead I suggested an ARM, for two reasons. First, Marisa was a "short-timer", even though she was planning to stay in the home for many years. The mortgage would be in place only a very few years. Yet the interest Marisa would save with an adjustable rate loan could be significant during at least the first couple of adjustment periods – and that might be as long as she planned to keep it anyway. Second, Marisa wanted to pay down her loan whenever she received a lump sum of cash, from the sale of her home or from her bonus checks. With a fixed-rate loan she could keep right on making huge lump-sum payments and yet her monthly payment would remain exactly the same until the loan was actually paid off. On the other hand, with an ARM loan, the payments would be re-amortized at each adjustment date. So any large, lump-sum payments would produce lower monthly payments after the loan was adjusted. That's one great thing about ARMs: the economy may control your interest rate, but you can adjust the size of your payments by speeding up the payback.

Advantages Of An Arm

- Lower interest rate (at least initially) than that for a fixed-rate loan.

- Lower monthly payments initially.

- Lower income needed to qualify (in most cases).

- If interest rates decline, so will an ARM's rate.

- You can often reduce the size of your payments at the next adjustment by paying extra. (This may be offset by a higher rate, though.)

Disadvantages Of An Arm

- Unpredictability of interest rate and payments.

8

Two-Step Loans

> *A Two-Step Loan is an adjustable-rate loan that adjusts only once during its 30-year term, usually after 5 or 7 years.*

You don't get free dancing lessons with this loan, although the name has a kind of toe-tapping catchiness to it. What you do get is fairly conservative financing that's slightly more affordable than a fixed-rate loan and a little less risky than the standard 1-year ARM or a balloon mortgage loan. The Two-Step is a recent hybrid that adopts features from each of these other loans. It can't seem to decide whether it's an adjustable or a fixed-rate loan, but straddles the fence between the two very nicely.

Like an adjustable-rate loan, the Two-Step has an initial interest rate based upon an index and a margin. The rate will usually be higher than that on a 1-year ARM but slightly lower than that on fixed-rate loans (perhaps a savings of about 1/2 to 3/4 of 1%). There are two common forms of Two-Step: one adjusts after 5 years, the other after 7 years. At the time of adjustment, the interest rate will be determined by the sum of the index rate as it stands then plus the margin. The new payment will be based on the new interest rate, the remaining loan balance and the remaining term of the loan. As in other ARMs, there is usually a lifetime cap to protect the borrower from an enormous interest increase. From the time of adjustment on, the rate will remain at the adjusted level and the loan will behave in every respect like a fixed-rate loan.

Two-Steps are excellent for borrowers who plan to stay in their home close to the 5- or 7- year time limit or for those who will be making larger payments to reduce the principal during the early years of the loan. As in the standard ARM loan, it's possible to reduce the monthly payments in the second step by lowering the principal balance significantly before the adjustment.

Advantages Of A Two-step Loan

- Initial payments are lower than those on a 30-year fixed-rate loan.

- Therefore qualifying is easier.

- When the principal balance is significantly reduced during the first step, it's possible to have lower payments during the second step (depending, of course, on the index).

Disadvantages Of A Two-step Loan

- There is no way to predict what the interest rate will be upon adjustment.

- The Two-Step is not as "affordable" as certain other loans, such as the 1-year ARM.

9

Loans with Buydowns & Discount Points

> *A Buydown is a sum of money paid to the lender at time of closing, in exchange for a reduction in the interest rate of the loan. In effect, a buydown is a form of prepaid interest. Ditto for Discount Points.*

$\mathbf{A}$ buydown is a handy little technique that makes a loan more affordable. With the lowering of the interest rate comes a lower monthly payment and many lenders will use that lower payment as a basis for qualifying the borrower. That means less income is needed to qualify for the loan. Or to put it another way, borrowers would be able to obtain a larger loan than they would have without the buydown.

Sellers, too, should consider the advantages of buydowns. As long as the buyer brings the required minimum amount of cash to the transaction, most lenders will permit anyone to pay the buydown fee: buyer, seller, parents, relatives or fairy godmother. It's a great selling tool in a sluggish real estate market. If a seller is willing to pay for a buydown, the number of potential buyers increases for each percentage point the interest is bought down. On a $100,000 loan at 10%, for example, bought down to reduced to 9%, a borrower would need to earn approximately $3100 less per year to qualify for the loan. That same 10% loan bought down to 8% would allow a buyer earning $6100 less per year to purchase the home. A buydown will dramatically increase a buyer's purchasing power and a seller's chances of a sale.

Two Kinds of Buydowns

There are two kinds of buydowns, permanent and temporary. A *permanent buydown* is one in which the interest rate remains at a constant low level for the entire term of a fixed-rate loan. Permanent buydowns are also available on some adjustable-rate loans; here the buydown affects the margin for the entire term of the loan. A *temporary buydown*, in comparison, changes the interest rate for only a short time, usually one to three years. After that, the rate returns to its original pre-buydown level, or in the case of an adjustable-rate loan, to the level it would have reached without the buydown.

Although a buydown is not a loan in itself, it may be used in combination with many different types of loans, from fixed-rate to adjustable, from conventional to government-backed. Most lenders offer a variety of buydown choices and an impressive assortment of loans to use them with. The result is a loan that's personally designed for you. How much will it cost? Because the costs of both types of buydowns are calculated differently, we'll take a closer look at each.

Permanent Buydowns

You would expect a 1% permanent buydown on a 30-year loan to be more expensive than a 1% temporary buydown lasting only three years. It is, but certainly not ten times the cost, even though it has ten times the duration.

Calculating a Permanent Buydown: Lender's Way

Both buydowns are a form of prepaid interest. In each case the lender calculates the amount of interest the borrower would have paid without the buydown and subtracts the interest paid with the buydown. However, this is not the actual cost of the buydown. Since the lender is going to collect the money up front and invest it, he will be earning money on that investment. Therefore, it is not necessary to collect the entire interest difference in cash at closing. The lender will use a 'yield chart' to determine how much money, when invested, will yield the amount of interest 'lost' by the buydown.

Calculating a Permanent Buydown: The Easy Way

Here's a rule of thumb that will give you an estimate of the cost:

For permanent buydowns, estimate a fee of approximately 6% of the loan amount for each 1% reduction in the interest rate. For example, the fee to buy down the interest rate on a $100,000 loan from 10% to 9% for the entire term of the loan would cost approximately 6% of $100,000, or $6000. The cost of buying down the interest rate on that same loan from 10% to 8% (a 2% reduction) would be twice the fee for a 1% permanent buydown, or 12% of the loan amount. On the $100,000 loan, that would amount to $12,800. Pretty costly! Although the expense involved will usually set a limit on the size of the buydown, some loans, especially those with a high LTV, come with additional restrictions. Check with your loan officer to see which loans are eligible for the size of permanent buydown you want.

Permanent Buydown with an Adjustable-Rate Loan

The terms 'permanent' and 'adjustable' may seem incompatible. But one constant in an adjustable-rate loan is the margin; it always remains the same. On an adjustable-rate loan with a margin of 2.75, for example, the interest rate will always be set 2.75% higher than the index rate. A permanent buydown can be used to reduce the margin. While the interest rate will still change as the index changes, a 1% permanent buydown would mean that the borrowers will always pay 1% less than they would have without the buydown. In our example, the margin would be reduced to 1.75%. The cost of a permanent buydown on an adjustable-rate loan is calculated by the same method we used for the fixed-rate loan. For each 1% reduction in the margin, estimate a fee equal to 6% of the loan amount.

Temporary Buydowns

Temporary buydowns come in quite handy when a borrower can't quite qualify for the loan. A short-term reduction in the interest rate, plus the lower monthly payments that go along, will often lower the amount of income needed to qualify for the loan. But be aware that this is not true for all buydowns. In some cases, the lender will use the pre-buydown rate to qualify the borrower, so be sure to inquire. Most temporary buydowns last only a few years; some are as short as one year. One-, two-, or three-year buydowns are the most commonly found.

There is plenty of choice in interest rates, too. Temporary buydowns may lower the rate in one of two ways. For a *flat-rate* temporary buydown, the interest rate when lowered stays the same throughout the buydown period. With a *graduated* temporary buydown, the interest rate starts low and gradually increases until it is back up to the pre-buydown level. We'll study each type separately.

Calculating the Temporary Buydown Fee: Flat Rate

A flat-rate temporary buydown works like this: a 2% 3-year buydown on a 10% fixed-rate loan will lower the interest rate to 8% for the first three years. From then on, the rate will remain at 10%. On an adjustable-rate loan, the length of a temporary buydown usually may not be longer than the period of adjustment. (And many lenders do not allow buydowns at all on ARMs with an adjustment period of less than three years.)

To calculate the cost of a temporary flat-rate buydown, simply add up the interest that will *not* be paid as a result of the lower rate. This method is not exact but should produce a reasonably close estimate of the buydown fee. Here is an example using a $100,000 loan at 10%, with a 2% buydown for two years. Using the amortization chart at the end of the book, determine what the monthly payment would be at 10% and, with the buydown, at 8%, then subtract.

	Loan Amount	Interest Rate	Monthly Payment
Without Buydown	$100,000	10%	$878
With Buydown	$100,000	8%	$734
Subtract to find the difference:			$144

That difference, $144, is the extra monthly interest that would be "saved" with the buydown. If we multiply it by the number of months the buydown remains in effect, we get the approximate cost of the buydown. Since our example is a two-year buydown, we will multiply $144 by 24. This buydown will cost approximately $3456.

Calculating the Temporary Buydown Fee: Graduated Rate

Graduated Buydowns have interest rates that start low and gradually increase until they reach the pre-buydown rate. There are a number of different interest rate combinations possible. Throughout the '80s, the most common graduated buydown was what is known as the 3-2-1. The interest rate is reduced 3% the first year, 2% the second, and 1% the third. From the fourth year on, it remains at the regular pre-buydown rate. With the tighter lending requirements in recent years, a shorter, shallower buydown, the 2-1, has become popular. It reduces the rate by 2% the first year, 1% the second, and goes back to the note rate on the third. Lenders (and the secondary market investors who buy their loans) have become very nervous about steep, quick payment increases. They'll still allow 3-2-1 buydowns but will often qualify the borrower on the rate that's 2% lower, rather than 3%. If you're considering a buydown, be sure to ask what interest rate will be used to qualify you.

Other buydown combinations are the 3-3-1, the 3-1-1, the 3-1, the 2-2-1 and the 2-1-1. Many lenders allow borrowers to design buydowns that meet their needs; other lenders offer only certain combinations. There may be restrictions on the size, the length or the pattern of graduated buydowns, and these will vary from loan to loan. Often borrowers seeking loans over 90% LTV will be limited to a two-year rather than a 3-year buydown, but this is not true of all loans.

If you thoroughly enjoy math, the fee for a graduated buydown may be calculated the same way we estimated a flat-rate buydown. Be sure to figure the cost of each interest step separately, then add your answers to give you the grand total. But again, there's an easier way. Use this handy chart to give you the approximate cost of a graduated buydown, keeping in mind that fees vary somewhat from lender to lender.

Cost of a Graduated Buydown	
Type of Buydown	Estimated Buydown Fee
3-2-1	.055 x the amount of the loan
3-3-1	.064 x the amount of the loan
3-1-1	.046 x the amount of the loan
3-1	.037 x the amount of the loan
2-2-1	.046 x the amount of the loan
2-1-1	.037 x the amount of the loan
2-1	.028 x the amount of the loan

Using the chart, we can calculate the cost of a 3-2-1 buydown for a $100,000 loan:

$100,000
x .055
_____
$ 5,500

Discount Points: A "Hidden" Buydown

Discount points, often known as "points", were once used primarily with FHA and VA loans but today are commonly found on most conventional loans. They are a form of prepaid interest, charged by the lender at closing. Each point costs 1% of the loan amount. By paying the cost of the discount points, a borrower effectively reduces the interest rate on the loan. (Usually either the seller or the buyer may pay the discount fee.) A lender, for example, may offer one 30-year fixed-rate loan at 10% interest, a 3% loan fee and no discount points. (That's known as the *par rate.*) A similar loan from the same lender might be available at 9.5% interest, with the same 3% loan fee, but with 2 or 3 discount points in addition to the fee. The payment of the points is actually reducing the interest rate in this case by one-half of 1%.

These days, you can custom-tailor your home mortgage loan to fit your specific needs. Do you have extra cash, but an income a little too low to qualify? Simply pay more discount points to get a loan with a lower interest rate. Do you have a good income but are short of cash? "Buy up" the rate—accept a loan with a higher interest rate, in exchange for no discount points. Or accept an even higher rate as a trade off for a loan at par plus a credit from your lender toward your loan costs.

Can you see that discount points are actually a form of permanent buydown? In Northwest lending offices today, you're very likely to encounter discount points on almost every loan. Buydowns, on the other hand, are pulled out of storage in emergencies, whenever it's necessary to beef up a borrower's qualifying power. As a matter of fact, the words "buydown fee" or "discount points" may not be used at all. Often the cost of the points is included in the loan fee quoted by a lender. If a loan officer mentions a fee that seems slightly higher than one charged by another lender, perhaps coupled with an interest rate that is a little lower, the fee quoted probably includes some built-in discount points to provide an attractive rate. That's one reason comparison shopping for loans can be so difficult. You'd like to compare apples to apples but if you shop for a low interest rate alone, without considering discount points and loan fees, you're not making a valid comparison.

Advantages of a Buydown or Discount Points

- Lower monthly payments, initially or for the term of the loan.

- Lower income needed to qualify for the loan. (Often true, but not always the case.)

- Borrower may often obtain a larger loan.

- Relatives, friends or the seller may be permitted to pay all or part of the fee, reducing the borrower's expense.

- Increased saleability when seller offers a buydown.

Disadvantage of a Buydown or Discount Points

- The only disadvantage of a buydown or discount points is their cost, which must be paid in cash at closing. On refinances, discount points may be financed with the loan.

10

Hybrids & Other Loans

The loans you have met so far are the types most commonly offered today by conventional lenders in the Pacific Northwest, but there are others you may possibly see in a lending office. To round out your knowledge of home mortgage financing, three are included here: the Graduated-Payment Loan, the Wrap or Blend Loan, and the Growing Equity Mortgage Loan. Two of the three are loans I would *not* recommend; in fact, that's one reason you'll find them in this book.

Graduated-Payment Loans (GPMs)

> *A Graduated-Payment Mortgage Loan is a fixed-rate loan which has monthly payments that start at a lower-than-normal level and increase at specified intervals during the first few years of the loan.*

In the realm of real estate loans, it's often a case of "here today, gone tomorrow." When the GPM faded from prominence in the loan market in the last few years, there were very few tears shed. Although it was designed to be an "affordable" loan, the side effects often killed the patient. That's why I was surprised to see the GPM being touted recently by one major lender. FHA and VA loan programs officially include the GPM as a standard loan, although most lenders don't offer it. But because you may encounter it, the GPM rates a mention here, along with a word of warning and the note that there are other ways to achieve affordability.

How a GPM Works

At first glance, a graduated-payment loan looks like a graduated buydown. There are the same low initial payments and the same gradual payment increases. What's missing in the GPM is the buydown fee. Then is this simply a free buydown? Not at all. While a buydown is paid for up front, at closing, the GPM is paid for during the term of the loan. Let's take a closer look at the GPM. The initial payments are much lower than those on a standard fixed-rate level-payment loan. In fact, they are too low to cover all of the interest that is due, so that means that there is nothing left over to apply to the principal. Therefore, the principal is not reduced, and we are also faced with the problem of unpaid interest. (The buydown fee would have covered in advance the cost of any unpaid interest.)

THE GRADUATED-PAYMENT LOAN

Deferred Interest

Lenders customarily defer the interest payment, adding it to the loan balance, where it will be paid over the term of the loan. This deferred interest, or "negative amortization" as it is often called, is one reason why GPMs have lost popularity. If property values should fall, deferred interest can be a problem. Borrowers have discovered that their loan balance, padded with the deferred interest, could exceed the market value of the home. It is hard to find a buyer for an $80,000 home financed by a $84,000 loan which must be assumed or repaid in full.

Note that the final level of monthly payments is higher than that for the standard level-payment loan. This is a result of two things: the higher loan balance, thanks to the deferred interest, and the shorter term at the time of the last increase. At each increase the payments are amortized over the remaining term of the loan; shorter terms bring higher monthly payments.

To avoid deferred interest, lenders prefer to use buydowns to provide the graduated-payment feature. Even though there are higher closing costs to face with a buydown fee, the safety factor may be well worth the price.

Advantages of a Graduated-Payment Mortgage Loan

- Low initial payments make qualifying easier.
- Borrowers can qualify for a larger GPM than for a standard fixed-rate level-payment loan.
- Interest rate is fixed.

Disadvantages of a Graduated-Payment Mortgage Loan

- Negative amortization (deferred interest) will increase the loan balance.
- Higher final monthly payments, as compared to standard fixed-rate level-payment loans.

63

Wrap Loans

> *A Wrap Loan, also known as a Blend Loan, is a mortgage loan that is "wrapped" around an existing loan. The lender assumes the existing first mortgage loan and supplies additional funds. The new interest rate will be a blend of the two rates.*

A Wrap Loan is similar at first glance to a land sales contract, but with an outside lender providing financing rather than the seller. The one essential ingredient in wrap loan financing is an underlying loan. (That, of course, is not true of a contract, which may be used with or without existing financing.) In addition, the underlying loan must be assumable. With a wrap, the lender assumes the existing loan, adds additional funds as needed and offers a new loan to the borrower at an interest rate that blends the rate of the underlying loan with the rate charged for the new funds.

Where to Obtain a Wrap Loan

With assumptions now on the list of endangered species, wrap loans are infrequently used today. Some conventional lenders offer a wrap only when they have financed the existing loan; others will wrap any assumable loan, no matter what its source. A few lenders will even wrap an assumable contract, if it is written to their specifications. Your real estate agent can help you find a lending institution or mortgage broker offering the kind of wrap loans you need.

Calculating the Interest Rate

Since a wrap loan is a blend of new and old funds, the resulting interest rate is also a blend of the two. Lenders use a special yield chart that takes into account the ratio of new money to old, the interest rate on the existing loan, and the yield required by the lender. Ask a loan officer to calculate the blended rate for your particular situation.

Many assumable loans are not worth wrapping. In general, the lower the percentage of new money required, the lower the rate on the underlying loan and the newer the existing loan, the more favorable the blended rate and monthly payments will be. The wrap loan will have a term that equals the term on the assumed loan. If, for instance, the underlying loan has 23 years left, the new wrap loan will also have a 23-year term. Payments will be amortized over 23 years, making them higher than payments on a 30-year loan at the same rate.

Wrap Loan vs Second Mortgage Loan

One advantage a wrap loan has over a second mortgage loan is the loan-to-value ratio. Because the lender has control over the underlying mortgage in wrap financing, the risk is reduced. Some lenders will loan as high as 95% LTV for a wrap, yet only 70% or 85% LTV on a second mortgage. Clearly this means that buyers with low down payments can often obtain a wrap loan, but not a second.

Advantages of a Wrap Loan

- Lower interest rate than on a standard new loan.

- Higher LTV ratios than on a second mortgage.

Disadvantages of a Wrap Loan

- Shorter amortization makes payments higher.

- Few assumptions produce good wrap loans.

Growing Equity Mortgage Loans

A Growing-Equity Mortgage (GEM) Loan is a fixed-rate loan with monthly payments that increase at regular intervals, resulting in an early payoff, rapid equity build-up and considerable interest savings.

You're not likely to encounter many GEM loans today in the Pacific Northwest, and for that I think we can give a

65

rousing cheer! While both FHA and VA officially list GEMs on their roster, most lenders haven't offered them recently. If you really want one (and I can't imagine why), your mortgage broker should be able to track one down for you.

Think of a GEM as an over-designed combination of a fixed-rate 15-year loan and a graduated-payment loan. Like the 15-year, it relies on increased monthly payments to achieve a rapid equity build-up. Like the GPM, it has stair-stepped payment amounts that start low (often much too low) and work their way up to lofty dimensions. Over the term of the loan, you'll save a significant amount of interest compared to a standard fixed-rate 30-year loan. But in the early years, when your payments are too low to cover the interest that's required, that interest will be deferred and you'll be faced with negative amortization, with its increasing loan balance.

GEMs are far too complicated for comfort and the deferred interest adds to the unappealing flavor of this loan. There are much better, and safer, ways to achieve the end results offered by a GEM. Consider, for example, a biweekly loan or a 15-year fixed with a buydown; it costs a little more up front (perhaps the seller will pay the buydown fee), but the there's no deferred amortization and you'll reap the full benefit of the interest savings.

Advantages of a Gem Loan

- Significant interest savings.
- The interest rate is fixed, not adjustable.
- The early payments are attractively low.

Disadvantages of a Gem Loan

- Many GEMs have deferred interest.
- The graduated payments end up considerably higher than those for level-payment loans.

Part III
GOVERNMENT
FINANCING

Part III

GOVERNMENT FINANCING

You've worked your way through the section of this book dealing with Conventional Financing. You've got the names and personality traits of the various loans down pat. Now it's time to add another dimension to the financing picture. We'll take those same basic loans and fit them into a whole new framework, that of government loans.

> A Government Loan is one which is either insured, guaranteed or funded by a department or agency of the government.

Northwesterners are fortunate to have a wide choice of government loans available for home financing. First, the federal government offers a splendid banquet of loans from the Department of Housing and Urban Development (FHA financing), VA loans from the Department of Veterans Affairs and rural housing loans from Farmers Home Administration. Then the state governments join the party, with loans from the Oregon Housing Agency, the Washington State Housing Finance Commission and, coming soon we hope, a new program from the Oregon Department of Veterans' Affairs. Adding to the richness and diversity of the menu are loans at the local level, too, as lenders follow the dictates of the Community Reinvestment Act and offer special financing to moderate income borrowers in mid-city neighborhoods.

If you're a member of a special interest group, a first-time homebuyer or veteran perhaps, or if your special interest is simply in finding good, affordable financing, read on to discover what government loans have to offer.

11

FHA Loans

The Federal Housing Administration (FHA) offers programs to insure home mortgage loans so that lenders can provide affordable financing with high loan-to-value ratios.

There are more FHA loans made each day than any other type of government loan. But don't expect to get a home mortgage loan from FHA, nor from HUD, the Department of Housing and Urban Development, which operates the FHA loan program. They're not lenders. Instead, HUD provides a mortgage insurance program for institutional lenders, giving them protection (and incentive) to make higher-risk loans: loans with a higher LTV ratio and easier qualifying ratios.

Since 1934 when the National Housing Act established it, FHA has been a leader in innovative home financing. Widespread use of the amortized loan, better home construction methods and the standardization of appraisal techniques are just a few of the results FHA has achieved since them.

Who is Eligible for an FHA Loan?

Anyone may apply for most FHA loan programs. Rich or less-than-wealthy, American citizen or not, there is a loan available to any U.S. resident who is a good credit risk and financially able to repay it. Recently there have been some tighter requirements applied. For example, non-owner occupants (in other words, investors) are not eligible for most FHA single-family financing. The one exception is the 203(k) program offering rehabilitation loans, as well as the HUD-owned properties acquired through foreclosure. The single-family programs that we see in residential real estate are tiny part of the total range of FHA financing, much of which is for large-scale development of affordable housing projects.

Where to Apply for an FHA Loan

Since HUD/FHA is an insurer rather than a lender, you must apply for a loan at a lending institution that handles FHA financing, not at HUD itself. You should have no difficulty finding a lender, since at least half of the Northwest's conventional lending institutions (banks, S&Ls, and mortgage brokers) also offer FHA real estate loans.

Some of these are what is known as *Direct Endorsement Lenders*. They have the in-house ability to process FHA loans, doing the appraisal and credit underwriting themselves, then applying to HUD/FHA for the insurance. This can save the borrower time, since documents do not have to be mailed to and from HUD for processing. Some Direct Endorsement Lenders, however, do not handle all of their loans internally. Questionable applications will often be sent to FHA for processing. Applying to a Direct Endorsement Lender is no guarantee for quick service on an FHA loan. More important is the efficiency of the loan officer and staff of the lending institution in preparing the necessary paperwork.

If you have difficulty locating a lender offering the FHA loan program you're interested in, contact the regional

HUD office serving your area, for the names of participating lenders:

Western Washington:

(except Clark-Skamania-Klickitat counties)

U.S. Department of Housing & Urban Development
Seattle Federal Office Building
909 First Avenue, Suite 200
Seattle, WA 98104-1000
(206) 220-5207

Eastern Washington:

U.S. Department of Housing & Urban Development
Farm Credit Bank Building, Eighth Floor
West 601 First Avenue
Spokane, WA 99204-0317
(509) 353-2594

Oregon, plus Clark County, WA:

(plus Clark-Skamania-Klickitat counties)

U.S. Department of Housing & Urban Development
Cascade Building
520 SW Sixth Avenue
Portland, OR 97204-1596
(503) 326-3077

Maximum Statutory Loan Limits

The maximum loan limits on FHA loans are set by Congress. They are adjusted by HUD to reflect local property values and are increased from time to time, as real estate prices rise. No matter which FHA loan program you choose, what the value of the home is, or what your financial capabilities are, your loan may not exceed your local limit. The following table shows the current maximum limits for each area in the Pacific Northwest:

FHA Loan Limits For Oregon & Washington

Lending Area	Single Family	Two Family	Three Family	Four Family
Chelan Co.	$ 77,900	$ 87,700	$ 106,600	$ 123,000
Cowlitz Co.	$ 75,250	$ 84,750	$ 103,000	$ 118,850
Clallam Co.	$ 106,400	$ 119,800	$ 145,600	$ 168,000
Douglas Co.	$ 83,600	$ 94,150	$ 114,400	$ 132,000
Grays Harbor Co.	$ 69,350	$ 78,100	$ 94,900	$ 109,500
Island Co.	$ 143,450	$ 161,550	$ 196,300	$ 226,500
Jefferson Co.	$ 124,875	$ 140,600	$ 170,200	$ 197,950
King Co./Seattle PMSA	$ 148,400	$ 167,150	$ 203,100	$ 234,350
Kitsap Co/Bremerton MSA	$ 113,950	$ 128,300	$ 155,900	$ 179,900
Lewis Co.	$ 79,350	$ 89,400	$ 108,600	$ 125,300
Mason Co.	$ 80,750	$ 90,950	$ 110,500	$ 127,500
Pierce Co./Tacoma PMSA	$ 105,450	$ 118,800	$ 144,300	$ 166,000
San Juan Co.	$ 151,725	$ 194,100	$ 234,600	$ 291,600
Skagit Co.	$ 104,500	$ 117,700	$ 143,000	$ 165,000
SnohomishCo./Seattle PMSA	$ 143,450	$ 161,550	$ 196,300	$ 226,500
Thurston Co/Olympia MSA	$ 102,100	$ 115,000	$ 139,750	$ 161,250
WhatcomCo/Bellingham MSA	$ 119,900	$ 135,050	$ 164,100	$ 189,350
Yakima Co./Yakima MSA	$ 83,350	$ 93,850	$ 114,050	$ 131,600
*Spokane Co./SpokaneMSA	$ 85,400	$ 96,150	$116,850	$ 134,800
** See below	$ 94,800	$ 106,750	$ 129,700	$ 149,650
*** See below	$ 67,500	$ 76,000	$ 92,000	$ 107,000
Jackson Co./Medford MSA	$ 90,750	$ 102,200	$ 124,150	$ 143,250
Lane Co./Eugene,Springfield	$ 89,000	$ 100,200	$ 121,750	$ 140,500
**** Portland metro area	$ 113,500	$ 127,800	$ 155,300	$ 179,200
All other OR counties	$ 85,200	$ 95,950	$ 116,600	$ 134,550

*   Plus Suncrest & Lakeridge Subdivisions.
**   Benton & Franklin Co's., Richland-Kennewick-Pasco MSA
*** Other Washington counties: Adams, Asotin, Columbia, Ferry, Garfield, Grant, Lincoln, Pend Oreille, Stevens, Walla Walla, Whitman.
**** Portland metro area, Clackamas-Columbia-Multnomah-Washington-Yamhill Counties (OR), plus Clark Co. (WA).

Interest Rates and Discount Points

Until November 1983, HUD established maximum interest rates for all FHA loans. At that time a law was signed giving lenders and borrowers the right to determine a rate for most FHA financing that is agreeable to them.

Since there is no longer one nationwide rate for a particular type of FHA loan, if you ask three different lenders what rate they charge, you'll get three different answers. In fact, you will probably hear at least three different rates from each institution. For example, one lender might offer FHA loans at 10%, 9.75% and 9.5%. Another will give a different range of numbers. Shop carefully. There are bargains available, but there are also hidden costs behind the interest figures. The 10% loan, for instance, will be accompanied by a smaller number of discount points than the 9.75% loan, and the 9.5% loan will have the largest number of points.

As in conventional financing, discount points are actually prepaid interest, with the cost of one discount point equal to one percent of the loan amount. It is certainly possible to obtain an FHA loan at "par rate", without discount points. But by paying discount points, you'll receive an interest rate that's lower than par. You'll find more about them in the chapter on Buydowns and Discount Points. At one time, FHA buyers were prohibited from paying the cost of the points. That was the responsibility of the sellers, as it still is for VA loans, Since 1983, however, either party may pay the points.

The FHA Mortgage Insurance Program

FHA mortgage insurance directly benefits the lending institutions that provide FHA loans. This insurance protects the lenders against the loss they would incur if foreclosure becomes necessary. Since statistics have shown that the higher the loan-to-value ratio, the greater the likelihood of default, common sense keeps lenders from loaning more than 95% of the value on conventional financing. With the FHA insurance, however, lenders feel safe in going even higher, in accordance with FHA guidelines. For some loans, such as the FHA veterans' loan, this can mean close to 100% LTV financing!

Calculating the Cost of FHA Mortgage Insurance

The FHA mortgage insurance program is funded by the borrowers, although sellers may pay the insurance premium if they wish to do so. Mortgage insurance is an unavoidable requirement on all FHA financing. For most FHA loans, the mortgage insurance premium (MIP) is calculated this way: first, there is an upfront mortgage insurance premium (called an UFMIP), which may be either paid in cash or added to the loan amount and financed. The UFMIP is now set at 3% of the loan amount for 30-year loans and 2% for 15-year loans. On most FHA loans there is also an annual premium, payable monthly, expressed as a percentage of the loan balance, then divided by 12 to determine the monthly insurance premium (MIP) amount. (See page 236 for the percentages used.) For example, a $65,000 30-year loan requires a $1950 UFMIP plus a $27 MIP added to the monthly loan payment.

Mortgage insurance on the most common FHA programs is calculated in this way. Unless otherwise noted in the specific loan program descriptions later in this chapter, the UFMIP/MIP method will apply. However, three of the programs outlined below, 203(k), 221(d)2 and 234(c), have no upfront MIP, simply a monthly MIP. An annual premium of 1/2 of 1% of the loan balance is divided by 12 and added to the monthly payment.

Qualifying Ratios Are Easier on the Borrower

The ratios (based on income and debts) that are used to determine whether the borrower is qualified for the loan are considerably higher than those used in conventional financing. This often makes it easier for a borrower to obtain a larger FHA loan (within the lending limits, of course) than conventional. Qualification ratios are explained in the chapter on Qualifying for a Loan, with worksheets to calculate maximum loan amounts for FHA and other financing.

Tax and Insurance Reserves

A reserve account for property taxes and homeowner's insurance is required on all FHA loans. In other words, the lender must pay the taxes and insurance directly, out of a fund established by the borrower at closing. The monthly payment on every FHA loan includes not only principal and interest, but also one month's worth of taxes and insurance. Reserve accounts are commonly found in conventional financing too, especially on loans over 80% LTV. With a lower LTV ratio on a conventional loan, the borrower has a choice of whether or not to have a reserve account. In FHA, the reserves are mandatory.

Assumability of an FHA Loan

One of the best reasons for choosing an FHA loan has lost a lot of its zing. In the past, FHA loans were assumable by either simple assumption or an assumption where the buyer was to required to qualify for the loan. The latter method resulted in a release of liability for the seller, the first method offered no release but certainly made a home easy to buy or sell. The choice was up to the seller. Today's new FHA loans are no longer assumable by simple assumption, although they are assumable with certain rstrictions. That's more than conventional lenders can offer today with fixed-rate loans. So there's still value in choosing an FHA loan for its assumability, even though we've now lost the best part of the package, from a buyer's or seller's standpoint. You'll find the FHA policy on assumptions, past and present, outlined in the chapter on Assumptions.

FHA Refinances

Many FHA programs may be used for refinancing an existing loan. Even investors may refinance an existing FHA loan under certain circumstances. You'll find the guidelines given in the chapter on Refinances, later in this book.

A Misconception About FHA

I have encountered dozens of homeowners who refuse at first to consider an FHA sale because they are convinced that they will be required to repaint the home from top to bottom, even if it is already in good condition. Or they are certain FHA will require a brand new roof, when a conventional lender will say the present one is just fine.

FHA is somewhat more stringent in certain respects, such as the necessity for adequate insulation in the attic and a plastic sheeting vapor barrier in the crawl space, but it's not excessively more rigid than today's conventional lending requirements.

FHA LOANS AT A GLANCE

	203b	203(b)2	203k	221(d)2	234(c)	245(a)GPM	245(a)GEM	251
Single-family home	X	X	X	X	X	X	X	X
Duplex to four-plex	X	X	X	X		X	X	X
Owner-occupied	X	X	X	X	X	X	X	X
Non-Owner-occupied		X						
Refinances	X		X		X			X
Existing Construction	X	X	X	X	X	X	X	X
New Construction	X	X		X	X	X	X	X
Manufactured Housing	X	X		X		X	X	X
Lender Sets Interest Rate	X	X	X	X	X	X	X	X
Fixed Rate	X	X	X	X	X	X	X	
Adjustable Rate								X
Level Payments	X	X	X	X	X			
Negative Amortization						X		
UFMIP & Monthly MIP	X	X				X	X	X
Monthly MIP only			X	X	X			
Buyer may pay Points	X	X	X	X	X	X	X	X
Buydown Permitted	X	X	X	X	X			

Types Of FHA Loans

The types, sub-types and intricate details of FHA financing could fill several volumes. Included here are the basic guidelines for FHA's current single-family loan programs offered by lenders in Washington and Oregon. The chart shows at a glance the wide range of loans. Some, such as the 203b, are offered by most FHA lenders. Yet for some of the little-used programs, it may be difficult to find a lender willing to provide them.

Since the FHA loans are similar to the conventional loans discussed earlier in this book, turn back to that section for information about the basic loan types, such as fixed-rate, adjustable-rate, and graduated-payment loans. As you study this chapter, please remember that loan limits and policies are subject to change by HUD/FHA.

SECTION 203b: The Basic FHA Loan

This loan, known as the 203b, is the most common of the FHA programs. It is a standard fixed-rate loan with a maximum term of 30 years. 15-year terms are also offered by many lenders. The 203b may be used to buy or refinance one- to four-family homes and mobile homes on owned (not rented) lots. New loans and refinances are available for occupant-borrowers; refinances are also available for non-occupant-borrowers, but with certain restrictions. (See the chapter on Refinances for details.)

Calculating Your Maximum 203b Loan

Applying the LTV and calculating your maximum loan amount used to be easy enough to calculate in your head, but no longer. While not difficult, it now requires two different computations.

First calculation:

1. Start by estimating your closing costs, using the worksheet on page 216 and the estimated figures from the chapter on Closing Costs. (You'll be permitted to include up to 100% of your closing costs in your calculations).

2. Add this to the sales price of the home or to the appraised value, whichever is less.

3. If the sales price (or appraisal) is $50,000 or less, multiply your total from step 2 by 97%. If the sales price is over $50,000, calculate 97% of the first $25,000, 95% of that between $25,000 and $125,000 and 90% of the balance to find your maximum loan limit for the first calculation.

Second calculation:

1. Start with the sales price or value given in the appraisal, whichever is less.

2. If the seller or a third party will be paying any of your closing costs (from the table on page 216), deduct these from the sales price (or appraised value). If the seller will not be paying any of your costs, use the sales price or appraised value in step 3.

3. If the sales price (or appraised value) is $50,000 or less, multiply your answer from step 2 by 98.75%. If the sales price (or appraisal) is over $50,000, multiply your answer in step 2 by 97.75%. Your answer is your maximum loan limit based on the second calculation.

Compare the answers from your first and second calculations. The lower of the two, rounded down to the nearest $50, is your FHA maximum loan amount.

SECTION 203(b)2: Veteran Loan

This loan, also known as the FHA/VA loan, is similar to the 203b, but is restricted to qualified veterans who wish to finance owner-occupied, single-family property for their principal residence. Mobile homes permanently placed on individual (owned) lots are also included. Veterans are limited to one of these high-ratio loans at a time, but are allowed to use this program as many times as they wish. To be eligible for a FHA/VA loan, a veteran must have served at least ninety days of active duty and must obtain a Certificate of Veteran's Status from the Department of Veterans Affairs. It's interesting to note that FHA is less restrictive than VA in the matter of veterans' eligibility; a World War I vet I know was able to obtain this loan, (at an age of over 80!); veterans from that war are not eligible for VA financing.

The maximum loan amount, term of the loan and mortgage insurance are identical to those of the 203b. Refer back to those sections for details. What does vary is the loan-to-value ratio, a more generous ratio for veterans:

Loan-to-Value Ratio for Veterans

1. The standard loan-to-value ratio for FHA/VA loans is 100% of the first $25,000 of FHA's appraised value including closing costs, then 95% of the amount from $25,000 to $125,000 and 90% of the remainder.

2. For new construction less than one year old, the maximum LTV is 90% of the FHA value plus closing costs.

3. Mobile homes on owned lots will qualify for the high LTV ratio only if they have been permanently situated for more than one year or are proposed construction to be built to HUD guidelines. All others will have a maximum LTV of 90%.

SECTION 203(k): Rehabilitation Loans

The FHA 203k loan allows a borrower to finance the purchase of a "fixer-upper" plus the cost of repairs necessary to bring it up to FHA standards. With other types of financing, any problems must be corrected before closing; with the 203k, the closing may take place before rehabilitation has begun. Funds for the repairs will be held in escrow and released as each phase of the work is completed.

It has been difficult in the past to find a lender willing to provide 203(k) financing. The paperwork is considerable and many institutions would rather not tackle it. But I'm happy to report that this program has undergone a recent revival and lenders in both Seattle and Portland are offering these loans. In other areas of the Pacific Northwest, the 203(k) may not be easy to find; contact the regional HUD office for the names of lending institutions handling the program.

Existing one- to four-unit homes are eligible for 203(k) financing (or refinancing). They may be either owner- or non-owner occupied. There is a minimum $5000 requirement for improvements or rehabilitation. These must follow HUD's specific guidelines and may not include luxuries like hot tubs or saunas.

Calculating Your Maximum 203(k) Loan

The maximum loan-to-value ratio on a 203(k) is different from that on the 203(b) loan. Here's how to calculate your maximum 203(k) loan:

1. Decide which is the lesser (this is known as the "HUD Value"):

   a. The HUD appraised as-is price plus HUD's estimate of rehabilitation costs, including 100% of the borrower-paid closing costs.

   b. Or, 110% of HUD's value after rehabilitation, including allowable closing costs.

2. Determine what is known as the "Aquisition Cost" by totaling your sales price, HUD's estimated rehabilitation cost, plus 100% of your closing costs (those actually paid by you, the borrower, not those paid for you by the seller).

3. Which is lesser, the HUD Value, or the Acquisition Cost? Use that figure to calculate your maximum loan amount: 97% of the first $25,000 and 95% of the remaining amount for owner-occupied homes; 85% of the lesser of the HUD Value or Acquisition Cost for investor loans.

Mortgage Insurance on a 203(k)

Mortgage insurance is paid monthly, with no Upfront MIP. The annual charge is 1/2 of 1% of the loan amount; divide by 12 for the monthly premium.

SECTION 221(d)2 LOANS: Low/Moderate Income

There are two reasons why this loan program is not often used. First, the loan limits are very low: for a single family home, from $36,000 to $42,000 (the higher amount for a 4-bedroom home and a family of five); duplex, $42,000; triplex, $57,600; fourplex, $68,400. Second, a city code inspection must be made, and electrical and plumbing inspections may also be required. If the code inspector finds evidence that the home does not comply with code standards, the owner must make the necessary repairs, even if the loan is not granted. This is not a popular program with sellers!

It's possible to include rehabilitation costs in the loan amount. Your maximum loan will be the lesser of 100% of HUD's appraised value (or sales price if lower) plus allowable closing costs, or 97% of the sum of value, closing costs and prepaid expenses (or acquisition if lower). Families displaced by urban renewal may qualify for higher LTVs. Mortgage insurance is paid monthly, at the rate of 1/2 of 1% of the loan amount per annum. Refinances are not available.

SECTION 234(c): Condominium Loans

Section 234(c) is a program that is used in conjunction with the standard FHA loans to finance (or refinance) new or existing condominium units that have been approved by FHA, VA or FNMA. The maximum loan limits and LTV are calculated according to the loan program that is being used in conjunction with the 234(c), usually 203(b). Mortgage insurance premiums are paid monthly, as described earlier in this chapter, with no Upfront MIP. There are additional guidelines for this loan relating to the percentage of owner-occupancy. You'll find that explained in the chapter on Financing A Condominium.

SECTION 245(a): The Graduated-payment Loan

The 245(a) was a popular FHA loan program when interest rates were high, in the early '80s Today, it's rarely used, but technically still available if lenders choose to offer it. If you've read about graduated payment loans (in the Conventional Loans section of this book), you'll understand why this loan is not likely to win a popularity contest. Like other GPMs, it has a fixed rate of interest and monthly payments that start at a lower level than those of a standard amortized loan. The payments are increased at specific intervals (in this case, yearly) until they reach a level which will pay off the loan in a total of thirty years. Five payment plans are available, with varying degrees of payment increase. Like other GPMs, it has deferred interest (negative amortization), since the early payments are too low to pay the amount of interest that is due. Because of this, a larger down payment is required that for the 203(b). This fixed-rate, graduated-payment loan may be used only for the purchase of an owner-occupied single-family home (including mobile homes on owned lots).

Under Section 245 in HUD's roster, there is also a growing-equity mortgage (GEM) loan, but lenders are not currently loaning under this program in the Pacific Northwest. For more information about GEM loans, see the chapter on Hybrids and Other Loans.

SECTION 251: Adjustable-Rate Mortgage Loans

HUD introduced the 251 ARM loan, with plenty of hoopla, in August 1984. Its reception by the lenders was frosty, but it later became widely accepted. The Section

251 program is an adjustable-rate loan, using as its index the weekly yield on one-year U.S. Treasury Constant Maturities. It has annual rate adjustments, with an annual cap of 1% and a lifetime cap of 5%. Loans are available for owner-occupied property only, new or existing single- to four-family homes, mobile homes and condominiums. Refinances are permitted.

Manufactured Housing Loans

Manufactured housing built after June 15, 1976 and permanently sited on land that is owned by the borrower is considered real property and is financed by the standard FHA home loans discussed above. But HUD also has other loan programs for mobile homes that will be placed on rented lots. you'll find more information about these and other loans in the chapter on Manufactured Housing.

Home Equity Conversion Mortgage (HECM)

Otherwise known as a Reverse Annuity Mortgage, this special program has a chapter all its own, later in this book. The HECM allows homeowners 62 or older to convert the equity in their homes to cash.

Advantages of FHA Financing

- Higher LTV ratio than conventional financing.
- Higher qualifying ratios.
- Even fixed-rate loans are assumable.
- Unlike VA loans, points may be paid by either party.

Disadvantages of FHA Financing

- Maximum regional loan amounts are lower than conventional limits.
- Mortgage insurance is required on all loans.

Special Loans From Local Sources

If you are looking for affordable financing and are having difficulty getting into a home of your own, take a look at some of the special loans offered by local lenders in various communities in Oregon and Washington. The Community Reinvestment Act requires lenders to make public details about where their loans are being made. As a result, there has been attention paid by lenders to areas previously "underloaned". Many banks are providing loans with special down payment assistance for borrowers whose income falls below the designated limits and who are purchasing a modest home in these specific neighborhoods. In addition, a number of community development agencies and private nonprofit groups undertake housing rehabilitation projects which can provide homes for moderate-income borrowers and a means to finance them.

Sometimes it is difficult to locate these sources of special loans. Consult the telephone directory for community development agencies in your area. If you live in Spokane or Portland, you're fortunate to have a referral agency to counsel and direct you to the appropriate financing:

Spokane Neighborhood Action Programs
Housing Resource Office
South 500 Stone
Spokane, WA 99202
(509) 456-7105

Portland Housing Center
2755 NE Broadway
Portland, OR 97232
(503) 282-7744

12

VA Loans

The U.S. Department of Veterans Affairs offers a loan guaranty to lenders who provide attractive lower-interest, often no-down-payment loans to qualified veterans.

If you are a veteran and want to finance a home, pay particular attention to the three loan programs designed especially for you: the FHA/VA and the U.S. Department of Veterans Affairs programs, both established by the Federal government and, for Oregon vets, the Oregon State Department of Veterans' Affairs loans, which will be covered in another chapter. Of the three, the U.S. Department of Veterans Affairs (VA) program is the only one where it's possible to obtain a substantually-sized no-down-payment loan. Add to this the benefits of a lower-than-conventional interest rate, minimum closing costs and easier qualifying standards, and you will see why this is an excellent loan to consider.

The VA Loan Guaranty

VA offers only a loan guaranty, not the actual funds, to institutional lenders who provide the loans according to VA standards. Just as the FHA insurance program protects lenders against default, so the VA guaranty covers a lender's loss at time of foreclosure. This is not an insurance program and so there is no mortgage insurance premium to be paid. The only additional fee charged, above the 1% loan origination fee and standard closing costs, is a VA funding fee of 1.5% of the loan amount. This is reduced to 0.75% with a 5% down payment, and to 0.50% with a 10% down payment. (Exceptions: National Guard/Reservists are charged a 0.75% higher funding fee, while veterans eligible for VA Compensation for service-related disabilities, and unremarried surviving spouses of veterans who died from service related causes pay no funding fee. On some refinances, the fee is reduced.)

Veteran's Eligibility

The first step in obtaining a loan is to have VA determine your eligibility. If you meet the requirements, VA will issue a Certificate of Eligibility that will enable you to apply for a VA loan. (Note that FHA/VA and Oregon DVA loans have very different eligibility requirements.)

The number of days of active duty required by VA depends upon the dates of service. Here are the three service categories:

1. Wartime Service: If you served anytime during:

- World War II (September 16, 1940 to July 25, 1947)

- Korean Conflict (June 27, 1950 to January 31, 1955)

- Vietnam Era (August 5, 1964 to May 7, 1975)

- Desert Storm (August 2, 1990 or later; even if you were not actually sent to the Persian Gulf.)

You must have served at least 90 days of active duty and must have received other than a dishonorable discharge. The 90-day limit may be waived if you were discharged because of a service-related disability.

2. Peacetime Service: If your service fell entirely within one of these periods:

- July 26, 1947 to June 26, 1950
- February 1, 1955 to August 4, 1964, or
- May 8, 1975 to September 7, 1980 (if enlisted) or to October 16, 1981 (if officer)

You must have served at least 181 days of continuous active duty and received other than a dishonorable discharge. Again, that 181-day requirement may be shortened if you were discharged because of a service-related disability.

3. Recent Service: If you were separated from service which began after these dates:

- September 7, 1980 (enlisted personnel) or
- October 16, 1981 (officers)

You must have completed 24 months of continuous active duty or the full period (at least 181 days) for which you were called or ordered to active duty, and you must have received other than a dishonorable discharge; or you must have completed at least 181 days of active duty with a hardship discharge or a discharge for the convenience of the government. Alternatively, you must have been determined to have a compensable service-connected disability or have been discharged for such a disability.

Other persons may be eligible to receive a VA loan:

4. Service personnel currently on active duty, who have served at least 181 days on continuous active status, regardless of when the service began.

5. Unmarried surviving spouses of eligible persons who died as the result of service-connected injuries.

6. The spouse of an active-duty member of the Armed Forces listed for over 90 days as missing in action or a prisoner of war.

7. Certain U.S. citizens who served in the armed forces of a government allied with the U.S. in WWII.

8. Individuals who served in other organizations, services, programs and schools may be eligible. VA will determine if such service may qualify.

9. Persons who have honorably completed six years in the Reserves or National Guard.

To obtain a certificate of eligibility, request Form 26-1880 from the nearest VA office or from your loan officer. There are two Department of Veterans Affairs regional offices in the Northwest. For the state of Oregon plus the Washington counties of Clark, Klickitat and Skamania:

VA Regional Office
Federal Building
1220 SW Third Avenue
Portland, OR 97204
(503) 326-2471

For the remainder of the state of Washington:

VA Regional Office
915 Second Avenue, 12th Floor
Seattle, WA 98174
(206) 624-7200

If you cannot find your original discharge papers to accompany the completed form, ask a benefits counselor at the VA office to help you obtain a Certificate in Lieu of Lost or Destroyed Discharge.

Where to Apply for a VA Loan

Since the Veterans Administration is not a lender, you must apply for a loan at a lending institution that handles VA loans. This should be easy to do, since many conventional lenders (banks, S&Ls, mortgage companies and mortgage brokers) also offer both FHA and VA loan programs. The Department of Veterans Affairs regional offices will provide a list of names of local lenders if you are unable to find one near you.

Automatic Processing Program

Lenders process VA loans in one of two ways. Many institutions have the authority to handle the loans on an "automatic" basis. These lenders are able to make the necessary credit decision and may proceed with the loan closing without waiting for VA approval. Other institutions handle VA loans on a "prior approval" basis; they must send all the pertinent information to VA to be evaluated. If the loan package is approved, the lender receives a certificate of guaranty and the closing may then take place. Both types of lenders must order an appraisal from VA; the only difference is in the approval of the credit information. Automatic processing can save considerable time, but the efficiency of a lender is still the biggest factor in getting a loan closed quickly.

Entitlement: How Large a Loan?

VA does not limit the size of loan a veteran may receive. It does, however, limit the size of the loan *guaranty*. In case of foreclosure, the lender will be reimbursed only up to the amount of the guaranty. This, indirectly, limits the size of loan, since lenders are cautious about stepping out on a limb. VA loans with no down payment (that is, 100% LTV) are commonly offered in an amount four times the guaranty. With additional money as down payment, a borrower can receive a larger loan, according to the particular lender's policy.

Determining the Veteran's Entitlement

The size of the guaranty is known as the veteran's "entitlement," a standard amount which is established by the Department of Veterans Affairs. The original entitlement level was $2,000, but that amount has been increased several times and is now $36,000 for homes valued at less than $144,000 and $46,000 for homes appraised at values between $144,000 and $184,000. Using the guidelines above, we can determine that the maximum 100% LTV loan offered by most lenders will be four times $46,000, or $184,000. In no case may the loan amount exceed the value of the property or the purchase price, whichever is less. The value, as determined by the Department of Veterans Affairs, is the figure shown on the Certificate of Reasonable Value (CRV), which is the name given to the VA appraisal required with each loan application.

Each eligible veteran is allowed the full amount of the entitlement. When veterans receive a VA home loan, they "use" that entitlement. They may not receive another VA loan until one of two situations occurs. If the property is sold and the loan is paid in full or transferred to another eligible veteran who agrees to use his or her entitlement, then the original borrower's full entitlement can be restored and used for another loan. Restoration of entitlement doesn't occur automatically, however; the veteran must apply at a VA office to have the full entitlement reinstated.

But even without full entitlement, it may still be possible to get a VA loan. If Congress has increased the entitlement since the first loan was obtained, a veteran may receive new financing based upon the difference between the entitlement used previously and the new entitlement level. For example, a veteran purchasing a home in 1974 would have had a $12,500 entitlement. Even if a non-veteran had assumed the loan and had not as yet repaid it, the veteran would still have at least a $23,500 entitlement today ($36,000 - $12,500) and perhaps as much as a $33,500 entitlement. Most lenders would offer the veteran a new loan up to $94,000 loan for a home under $144,000, and a loan up to $134,000 for a home in the $144,000 to $184,000 range.

Interest Rate and Discount Points on VA Loans

Since October 1992, the Department of Veterans Affairs has allowed the interest rate for all VA loans to be negotiated by the borrower and lender, in the same way FHA and conventional rates are agreed upon, rather than being set by DVA. This has proved to be an advantage to borrowers for an interesting reason: discount points. VA buyers have been forbidden to pay the cost of discount points, and with a set interest rate, the discount points necessary to make the loans palatable to lenders were, at times, enough to frighten sellers away from accepting all VA loans (since they had to bear the cost). Now buyers may choose a loan without discount points (at a slightly higher interest rate) or one with the number of discount points the seller will agree to pay.

Unlike most FHA transactions, where either party may pay the discount points, VA still requires the seller to pay them, except in certain cases. One exception is for a refinance or home improvement loan. There the borrower may, and in fact, must pay the points. This particular feature of VA loans can make them less appealing to sellers, since the points will increase their costs. Keep this in mind if you are in the midst of a seller's market, where properties sell so quickly that sellers can be choosy. They'll be far more likely to pick a "cleaner" offer (one with no additional points to pay) and a VA offer that includes points will put you at a disadvantage.

Tax and Insurance Reserves

As with FHA financing, the monthly payment on a VA loan includes an additional amount to cover 1/12th of both the annual property tax and homeowner's insurance premium. Payment to the county tax office and the insurance company will be made annually by the lender.

Assumability of a VA Loan

In the past, one of the most appealing reasons for choosing a VA loan was its assumability. Before March 1, 1988,

VA loans could be assumed in one of two ways, via simple assumption or by an assumption where the new buyers are required to make formal application and qualify for the loan. (You'll find more about the different types of assumptions in chapter 19.) Loans obtained since that date, however, may not be assumed by a simple assumption. They may be assumed (by either vets or non-vets) by the second method only, a method that is not as attractive to buyers, of course. While the elimination of simple assumptions has reduced the attractiveness of VA loans, the remaining benefits of a lower interest rate, low or no down payment and easier qualifying make them an excellent way for veterans to finance a home.

Types of Loans Available

VA loans may be used to finance or refinance a home, both new construction and existing. Mobile home and condominium loans are also available. The veteran borrower must occupy the home within a reasonable amount of time after closing; non-owner-occupied property may not be financed. Loans for multi-unit buildings are available (up to a 4-plex for one veteran), but the veteran must occupy one of the units. Borrowers who depend upon rental income from the building to qualify for the loan must show proof that they have the background or skills to be a successful landlord, plus sufficient cash reserves to make 6 months of loan payments without the rental income.

VA guarantees several different loan plans— or at least technically offers them: the traditional fixed-rate loan, a an adjustable-rate loan, the graduated-payment mortgage (GPM) loan, and the growing-equity mortgage (GEM) loan. In recent years, the GPM and GEM loans have fallen out of favor with lenders and today very few, if any, lenders offer them. These loans are similar in structure to their conventional counterparts, and the adjustable-rate loan is quite like the FHA ARM, so be sure to study the Conventional Loans and FHA sections for the basic information about each method. Here, however, are the specific VA details.

VA Traditional Fixed-rate Mortgage Loans

The fixed-rate loans guaranteed by the Department of Veterans Affairs are standard loans with a maximum term of 30 years and 32 days. Recently, 15-year loans have become popular and are offered by many lenders.

VA gives lenders certain latitude in lending practice, provided minimum standards are met. For example, on a fixed-rate loan, VA does not require a down payment if the purchase price does not exceed the reasonable value of the property, yet a lender may ask for one. The lending institution around the corner may have a slightly different requirement and especially now that interest rates are negotiable, it will pay you to shop around. The traditional fixed-rate mortgage loan is widely available; it has long been the most popular type of VA financing.

VA Adjustable-rate Mortgage Loans

VA was the last of the major loan programs to offer adjustable-rate financing. You'll find VA ARMs available with an annual cap of 1% and a lifetime cap of 5%. When it comes to underwriting guidelines, DVA has taken a conservative approach to its adjustable-rate financing. Borrowers are qualified at the maximum second-year rate (1% above the initial rate). This assures VA that the borrowers will be able to handle an increased payment, if necessary.

VA Growing-equity Mortgage Loans

VA guarantees GEM loans, however you'll have a difficult time finding a lending institution offering one. An acceptable VA GEM must have payment increases that are moderate, for example, 3% per year for ten years; deferred interest is not permitted. These are typically based on 30-year terms, but the increasing payments lead to an early payoff, in roughly half the time.

VA Graduated Payment Mortgage Loans

There is one GPM plan approved for a VA guaranty but it is rarely, if ever, used today. This plan has annual loan payment increases of 7.5% for the first five years. From the sixth year, the payments remain level for the remaining term. It is a fixed-rate 30-year loan with initial monthly payments too low to cover the interest due, which means deferred interest and an increasing loan balance for the first few years of the loan.

Manufactured Housing Loans

Manufactured homes with permanent foundations on borrower-owned land are financed by the VA mortgage loans discussed above. VA will also guarantee loans for new or used mobile homes on rented lots, but at the present time, it is difficult to find a lender who will finance a used home.

Home Improvement Loans

VA home improvement loans are rarely written, although VA will guarantee second mortgage loans to qualified veterans. Few, if any, lenders here offer this program, preferring instead to use FHA or conventional plans.

Advantages Of VA Loans

- Low down payment or no down payment financing possible.
- Easier to qualify for than conventional financing (see the chapter on Qualifying.)
- VA loans are assumable.
- No mortgage insurance premium to pay, so monthly payments are lower.

Disadvantages Of VA Loans

- You must, of course, be a qualified veteran to obtain one.

13

FmHA Loans

Farmers Home Administration offers two loan programs: subsidized loans for low income borrowers and a guaranteed loan program for moderate-income borrowers. Both loans are for the purchase of modest homes in rural areas by buyers who are unable to obtain other financing.

If your family income meets the guidelines for this financing, and if you are looking for a modest home in a rural area or in a small country town, an FmHA loan may be just right for you. The Farmers Home Administration, an agency of the U.S. Department of Agriculture, offers a very wide range of credit programs to provide funds for rural projects that might be difficult to finance otherwise. The list is amazingly varied: In addition to home loans, there are loans for buying a farm, developing and conserving soil and water resources, forming a grazing association, building housing for farm laborers, and many other worthwhile projects. Here we are concerned with home financing and so we'll deal just with that particular area.

Home Financing with FmHA

· There are two very different housing loan programs available to buyers. For low and very-low income borrowers, FmHA funds its rural housing loans directly. Many of these are subsidized loans, with payments set at a level the borrower can afford. The second program is for moderate-income homebuyers; these loans are funded by private lenders, but guaranteed by Farmers Home Administration. The two programs differ widely in many requirements, but there are some points of similarity. First, the loans must be for the purpose of purchasing modest housing in a rural area. Second, borrowers must have a dependable income with a good credit rating and the ability to repay the loan. However, they must be unable to obtain a loan from another source. Finally, they must not already own an adequate home and must be prepared to occupy the home financed by an FmHA loan.

Which Homes Are Eligible?

The FmHA county offices have maps showing the geographical areas which are eligible for loans. These are usually open county areas or rural towns with a population of 10,000 or less (or up to 20,000 in certain areas near towns or cities). Bedroom communities or suburbs are not eligible.

The homes themselves must be adequate to meet the needs of the family but modest in size, design and cost. For example, under the direct loan program, existing dwellings for households of two or more members must contain not more than 1,300 square feet. Any extras that are not absolutely essential, such as additional bathrooms, family rooms or fireplaces usually will not be approved. The lot must be of a modest size also, limited to approximately one acre. (FmHA does finance farms, too, and questions concerning these loans should be directed to the local FmHA office.)

If you wish to have a home built, you may secure permanent financing through FmHA, but you must obtain a temporary construction loan from another source. You must find your own builder and have a set of plans available for FmHA approval.

How to Calculate Your Income Eligibility

Maximum income limits are set by the FmHA and are strictly followed. However, "Adjusted Income" is used rather than straight income. Here is how to calculate your Adjusted Income:

Take the total gross income (before taxes and deductions) of all the people who are living in the home. Subtract $480 for each minor child residing in the household and an additional $400 if the applicant or co-applicant is elderly, handicapped or disabled (one $400 deduction per family). The FmHA may also allow you to subtract the cost of certain job-related expenses, such as child-care costs. The amount remaining is your Adjusted Income.

Example: A family with a gross income of $30,000, two dependent children and a handicapped applicant:

Gross Income .... $30,000.
Less $480 per child ($480 x 2) .... $960.
Less $400 (disabled applicant) .... $400.

Adjusted Income .... $28,640.

To qualify for a loan, the applicant's Adjusted Income must not exceed the limits set by FmHA. These limits are adjusted frequently and vary with the location of the home and the number of household members; a household with one member will have a considerably lower limit than one with ten members. The income limits also differ with each of the two programs. Let's take a look at the specifics of each.

The Guaranteed Housing Program

Because this is a program for moderate-income borrowers, the income limits are higher than those for the Direct Loan Program. As an example, the maximum Adjusted Income in Washington for a family of four seeking a guaranteed loan currently ranges from $34,500 in many counties to a high of $50,750 in the Seattle area. In Oregon, the maximum Adjusted Income for a family of four now ranges from $34,650 in some counties, up to $45,300 in the Portland area. The family in our example above (with an adjusted income of $28,640) meets the income eligibility requirents in all Oregon and Washington counties, but it's possible that these borrowers may not be able to qualify for the non-subsidized guaranteed loan program, since their income may not be high enough to satisfy the qualifying ratios used by the lenders. (Use the FHA ratios in the worksheet on page 202.)

Just as the income limits vary with the geographical area, so do the maximum loan limits. They are roughly similar to those set by FHA (you'll find these in the table on page 72). However, there is often a time lag until FmHA catches up to FHA changes, so at any one time the FmHA loan limits may be somewhat lower than FHA's.

FmHA Guaranteed Loans are fixed-rate 30-year loans. They are available from participating lenders; for a list of lenders in your community, contact your local FmHA district or county office.

The Direct Loan Program

Funds are available directly from FmHA, for borrowers whose income falls at or below the "low" and "very low" income limits. In Washington, these maximum limits today range from $24,000 in several counties to $35,300 in the Seattle area. In Oregon, the range is from $24,100 to $31,500. FmHA allocates about 40% of all available funds for what are known as Very Low Income Loans, with maximum income limits set at approximately 62% of the Low Income limits.

An attractive feature of the direct loan program is the subsidized Interest Credit (I.C.) offered to borrowers whose income is too low to qualify for the regular monthly payment. The I.C. subsidy will reduce the monthly payment to a level that the buyer can afford, but the amount of the reduction will be added to the balance of the loan. That means it will eventually be repaid by the borrower when the home is sold. No down payment is required, except for any earnest money the seller might ask for. In other words, FmHA will finance up to 100% of the value of the home.

FmHA direct loans are fixed-rate loans with a maximum term of 33 years in most cases, but occasionally up to 38 years. Manufactured housing loans are limited to a maximum of 30 years. Funding for the program is allocated by Congress. The rates on the loans are usually lower than conventional market rates, with the I.C. subsidy providing even more favorable terms for those borrowers who qualify.

In Oregon or Washington, you can apply for a direct loan at the FmHA office that serves the county in which the home is located. To find the office you need, look in the phone book under the U.S. Department of Agriculture or contact your FmHA State Office for more information.

FmHA State Office, Oregon:

Farmers Home Administration, USDA
Room 1590, Federal Building
1220 SW Third Avenue
Portland, Oregon 97204
(503) 326-2734

FmHA State Office, Washington:

Farmers Home Administration, USDA
Room 319, Federal Building
P.O. Box 2427
Wenatchee, Washington 98807-2427
(509) 664-0240

Advantages of FmHA Loans

- Loans are available for those unable to find other financing.

- Payment subsidy for low-income borrowers.

- Up to 100% loan-to-value ratio on some loans.

Disadvantages of FmHA Loans

- Income limits may eliminate many borrowers.

- The home must be modest in size and amenities.

- It must be located in a designated rural area.

14

State Housing Loans

> *The Oregon Housing Agency and the Washington State Housing Finance Commission offer loan programs (and in Oregon, a tax credit program) primarily for first-time homebuyers.*

If you're looking for your first home and your income is at or below the median level for your state or county, here are two exceptionally fine loan programs that should be right at the top of your shopping list. Both Oregon's Single Family Mortgage Program and Washington's House Key Program were designed to help moderate income first-time buyers (or those who haven't owned a home in the past three years) become homeowners. Consider these two as "sister" programs: they're certainly not identical, yet since they have the same parent, the similarities are unmistakable.

Taking aim directly at the needs of first-time buyers, Congress has given states the authority to sell tax exempt mortgage revenue bonds for the purpose of funding affordable home mortgage loans for moderate income borrowers. To date, 49 of the 50 states have initiated such a program and here in the Pacific Northwest, the results keep getting better all the time!

Both the Oregon Housing Agency and the Washington State Housing Finance Commission offer 30-year fixed-rate loans to buyers who have not owned a home in the past three years and whose income does not exceed the current median income levels of their geographical area. The loans are processed and funded by participating lending institutions throughout each state, then purchased by the state housing agencies with bond sale funds. Certain guidelines for the program are dictated by Congress, then given their own unique identity by the states. Borrowers must be residents of the state at the time of purchase and must occupy the home as their principal residence. In areas designated as "Targeted Areas" (neighborhoods where the state wants to encourage market activity), the three-year previous ownership rule will be overlooked and higher purchase price and/or income limits are allowed.

Unlike the major federal programs, the money supply is not steady or predictable. States are allocated a limit on the total value of the bonds that can be sold; when the funds from a bond sale run out, there may be no additional funding until the next bond sale. It is left up to the states to decide how and when to use their allocation. There is no set date for bond sales, however each state aims toward a schedule of at least one per year, a second if the bond cap permits it. Watch for Oregon's bond sale in March or April, with often a second, smaller one in the fall; Washington's sale takes place in or around mid-July. Exact timing will depend upon bond market conditions.

Once the sale has taken place, an interest rate will be determined for the loans. Current maximum income limits and housing price limits will be established and participating lenders may begin to reserve funds for borrowers. To reserve funds, a borrower must have an accepted offer and must apply for a loan at the office of one of the lenders who have signed up to participate in that round of the program. A list of participating lenders is available from each state.

Oregon's Single Family Mortgage Program

In 1977, Oregon introduced "Loans to Lenders" (the predecessor of today's program), and has been offering loans ever since. Borrowers can choose from either the mortgage loan program, or the Mortgage Credit Certificate Program (MCC), which offers a tax credit on the borrower's federal income tax return. Some buyers find that the tax credit, used with other financing, is better suited to their needs than the loan program. Both are designed to make housing affordable for first-timers.

The loan program is now FHA-insured, which means that borrowers receive FHA 203(b) 30-year fixed-rate loans at lower-than-market interest rates. Today, the maximum income limits are $40,600 in the 5-county Metro Portland area and $35,600 elsewhere in the state. For MCCs, there are lower income limits for 1- and 2-person households, while those for a 3-person household match the income limits in the loan program. For both loans and MCCs, the maximum purchase price limits for existing homes in non-targeted areas range from $70,830 to $85,320 ($86,570 to $104,280 in targeted areas). For new construction, the limits are higher: $117,990 to $154,980 in non-targeted areas, $144,210 to $189,420 in targeted areas. Note that these limits may change with each bond sale.

For more information about Oregon's two programs, contact:

Oregon Housing Agency
1600 State Street, Suite 100
Salem, Oregon 97310
(503) 378-4343

Washington's House Key Program

The Washington State Housing Finance Commission has been busy since 1983 finding creative ways to make housing loans affordable for first-time buyers. Like Oregon's program, Washington offers FHA-insured 30-year fixed-rate loans at very attractive interest rates, but recently it also made available a conventional loan program, also at lower-than-market rates. (Your participating loan officer can help you decide which of the two programs would be better suited to your situation.) The state has discontinued its Mortgage Credit Certificates, preferring to channel the funds directly to the loan program.

At this time, Washington's maximum income limits for a household of 1 or 2 in a non-targeted area range from $37,500 to $43,500 (targeted area: $45,000 to $49,500). For a family of 3 or more, the non-targeted limits are $42,000 to $48,000 (with targeted area limits from $48,000 to $51,000). Current maximum purchase price limits on existing homes run from $73,000 to $130,000 (targeted area: $90,000 to $155,000). For new homes, the limits recently were the same for target and non-targeted areas: a range of $120,000 in some counties to $155,000 in the Seattle area. Remember that limits change with every bond sale. For more information, contact:

The Washington State Housing Finance Commission
1111 Third Avenue, Suite 2240
Seattle, Washington 98101-3202
(206) 464-7139

Advantages of State Housing Loans

- Excellent interest rate.
- Easier to qualify for than standard financing.

Disadvantages of State Housing Loans

- Funds are not always available.
- Income and purchase price restrictions apply.
- Low sales price limit plus moderate income limit.

15

Oregon
DVA Loans

The Oregon Department of Veteran's Affairs (ODVA) offers a program that includes both conventional and FHA loans for eligible Oregon veterans who are purchasing a primary residence in Oregon.

Sorry, Washingtonians, you'll have to skip this chapter. Here's a loan program that's for Oregonians only. Oregon is one of only five states to offer some form of home mortgage loan prgram for eligible veterans, not to be confused with the federal loan guaranty program run by the U.S. Department of Veteran's Affairs which is available to veterans in all fifty states.

For over 40 years, the Oregon Department of Veterans Affairs (ODVA) offered an mortgage loan program that was very appealing to veterans. Variable-rate loans at below-conventional rates proved to be a popular and effective way for Oregon's veterans to finance a home or farm property. Unfortunately, after the real estate slump of the '80s, the program ran into difficulties and ODVA stopped offering new loans.

In 1991, a new ODVA loan program got underway, offering veterans a choice of either FHA or conventional financing for the purchase of a home. These loans are financed by tax-exempt bonds issued by the State of Oregon and are available through participating lending institutions around the state, as well as through the ODVA central office in Salem.

Eligibility Requirements

Only veterans who live in Oregon at the time of loan application may apply for an ODVA loan. They must have served a minimum of 210 consecutive days of active service (unless they were released earlier because of a service-related disability). Part of this service must have occurred on or before December 31, 1976 (active duty for training is excluded) and they must have received an honorable discharge. In addition, they must have **either** entered active duty while a resident of Oregon **or** have been a resident of Oregon for at least five years after discharge from active duty. Veterans must apply for the loan within thirty years from the date of discharge.

Details About the Loans Offered

Financing is available for the purchase of single-family homes to be used as primary residences only— no rental property, vacation homes or refinances (with the exception of financing to replace certain short-term construction or temporary loans).

The maximum loan available is 90% of the purchase price or appraised value (whichever is less), and the loan may not exceed $80,000. An upfront mortgage insurance premium may be financed as long as the total loan does not exceed the $80,000 limit.

A choice of loan terms is offered, with the most common being 15- and 30-year terms.

Weatherization Requirements

Homes built before July 1, 1974 must meet the weatherization requirements developed by the Oregon Department of Energy, if they are to be financed by ODVA. Loans which include funds for weatherization may not exceed the maximum 90% LTV.

Where to Apply for an ODVA Loan

Before applying for financing, veterans should contact the ODVA office in Salem, request an Eligibilty Application Form 409-M and submit it with a copy of their DD-214 (separation or discharge report).

Once eligibility is established, the veteran may apply for a loan at the Salem ODVA office or at the office of any participating lender. A list is available from ODVA. Whether the loan is made at ODVA or at a lending institution, the same fees, costs, eligibility requirements and loan terms will apply.

For more information about this program, contact:

The Oregon Department of Veterans Affairs
Central Office
Oregon Veterans' Building
700 Summer Street NE
Salem, OR 97310-1201
(800) 382-7253 (toll-free within Oregon)
(503) 373-2062

ADVANTAGES OF ODVA LOANS

- Depending upon the timing of the bond sale and current market conditions, the interest rates offered on ODVA loans may be attractive, although this is not always the case.

DISADVANTAGES OF ODVA LOANS

- Loans are available only to eligible Oregon veterans.

- Down payment requirements are higher than those for standard FHA and conventional loans.

- Maximum loan limit is low.

Part IV
SELLER
FINANCING

Part IV

SELLER FINANCING

There are times and reasons for not using institutional financing. Maybe you and your loan officer can't quite come to an agreement regarding your ability to repay a loan. Could be that the home in question wouldn't fare any better under the scrutiny of the institutional lenders. Or maybe you're just one of those independent sorts who see no need to let a lender collect years of hefty interest payments. All of those are perfectly valid reasons for "going it alone".

Seller financing is not a new idea; in fact it's about as old as the subject of real estate financing gets. So after all this time, you'd think we'd have it down to a science, wouldn't you? Well, to judge from some of the fascinating tales of conflict and intrigue I hear on HOUSE CALLS, I think the message hasn't reached everyone yet. Seller financing can be an excellent way to buy or sell a home, if it's done with a good common sense and a healthy respect for professional assistance. Here's how!

16

Land Sales Contracts

A Land Sales Contract is a financing agreement between the buyer and seller of a piece of property. It differs from other forms of seller financing in that the seller usually retains legal title to the property until the buyer has made the final payment.

A well-known real estate writer once rated the land sales contract as the worst financing method around. I disagree wholeheartedly. It can be an excellent, inexpensive way to finance a home and if done with care, a contract will be a "win-win" transaction, with both buyer and seller benefiting. Land sales contracts aren't a recent innovation, even though they became very popular during the high-interest eighties, when few buyers were able to afford new institutional loans. People have been buying and selling homes on contract for centuries. In other parts of the country, you'll hear Land Sales Contracts called "land contracts," "contracts for deed" or "installment sales contracts"; the procedure is known simply as "buying (or selling) on contract."

How a Contract Works

Let's use an imaginary situation to illustrate a contract sale:

> Dottie and Roger Smith's home is for sale and they're asking $99,000. Two real estate agents show the home one day and, as luck would have it, both prospective buyers write offers to purchase. Offer number one is an all-cash offer of $93,000. The second offer is a full-price offer of $99,000. It offers $14,000 in cash as a down payment and asks the Smiths to carry a contract in the amount of $85,000 at 10% interest for 30 years. Which should the Smiths consider?

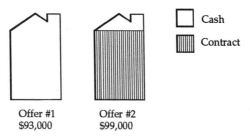

☐ Cash

▦ Contract

Offer #1   Offer #2
$93,000 $99,000

Which Offer Should the Smiths Consider?

Offer number one is a simple transaction with no strings attached. At closing, the buyers would pay cash, out of which the seller's closing expenses would be deducted, and the Smiths would receive the balance. They would give possession and legal title to the buyers and would have no further legal interest in the home.

Offer number two is for a higher price, as many contract transactions are, since the seller will be acting as lender. However, the Smiths would receive less cash at closing. Here the buyers and the sellers would enter into a contract agreement, drawn up by an attorney and signed by both parties. The buyers would pay the $14,000 cash plus their closing expenses. The sellers' closing costs and broker's fees would be deducted from the $14,000 and the balance would go to the Smiths.

According to the terms of the contract agreement, the new buyers would pay the Smiths $746.30 a month in principal and interest, and would pay the taxes and insurance when due. They would take possession of the home but would not receive legal title, the deed to the property, until the last payment has been made. This explains the term "contract for deed"; the buyer and seller enter into an agreement to transfer the deed when the contract terms have been met.

Dottie and Roger will have to decide whether to accept (or counter) the all-cash offer or to accept the contract offer with its small amount of cash at closing plus 10% return on the money they have invested in their home. They will base their decision on many factors. Do they need cash to buy another home? Is 10% a reasonable interest rate to earn? Is one offer better than the other from a tax standpoint? Are the buyers reliable?

No Such Thing as a "Standard" Contract

An important thing to remember is that a contract is simply a collection of points that both the buyer and seller agree to follow. It can be personalized by adding special provisions that are important to the parties involved. In the contract between the Smiths and the buyers, for example, the buyers may wish to have a statement included that allows the contract to be assumed by a new buyer if they should decide to sell. If the Smiths are in agreement, fine. If not, the sale cannot take place until a compromise has been reached.

Seek Professional Advice

You can, if you wish, walk into an office supply store and buy a blank contract form. There may be several varieties to choose from, each with a dizzying spread of small print and large words. But I cannot over-emphasize the importance of good legal advice for any contract sale. Yes, I'll be absolutely blunt about it: if you enter into a land sales contract without relying on the advice of your attorney, you are asking for trouble. Spend an hour or two listening to a few of the disaster stories I hear on HOUSE CALLS and you'll be convinced that, in a contract transaction, legal fees are money well spent.

Your attorney may choose to use or modify a blank form, or may type up a "from-scratch" version, but you can be sure that the end result will protect *your* interest in the property. Not all preprinted contract forms can make that claim. In fact, one attorney I know maintains that the blank contract forms often favor the rights of one party over another. If you aren't sure just what your rights are, can you recognize when they have been overlooked? Don't rely on the other party's attorney to draw up a contract that's especially congenial to you; retain your own lawyer to see to your interests. Most attorneys charge from $100 to $200 to draw up a simple real estate contract. Either the buyer or the seller may pay for the preparation; however, it's a good idea for the other party to ask his or her own attorney to review the contract after it is written and *before* it is signed.

Contract Provisions that Can Be Included

There are many provisions which should be included in a contract and others that are optional. It is wise to have the contract provisions also written into the original sales agreement (the offer to buy the property), although they can be added at the time the contract is prepared if both parties agree. Some provisions will appear in all contracts: the size, frequency and duration of the monthly payments, and how and when the taxes and insurance are to be paid. There should be default provisions, outlining a plan of action if either party fails to keep the agreement. In addition, there will be an agreement to convey the deed to the buyer at a specific time, usually when the final payment has been made.

The following provisions are optional, but are often used in contracts:

Balloon Payment: A balloon payment is a lump-sum payment of the principal amount. If the Smiths, in our example above, did not want to carry the contract for 30 years, they would have two options. First, they could amortize the payments over a shorter period of time, say 15 years, increasing the monthly payments from $746 to $914. That would be fine for the Smiths but it might be impossible for the buyers to pay that amount.

The second option is to add a balloon payment provision to the original offer. The payments could be amortized over a 30-year period, with payments of $746, but at the end of 15 years, the entire remaining loan balance would be due. In this case, $69,388 out of the original $85,000 would be owed to the Smiths. That means that the buyers would have to come up with $69,388 in cash to pay off the loan. Usually this is done by refinancing the home.

What happens if the buyers cannot get financing? As Shakespeare put it, "Ay, there's the rub." What does happen depends entirely upon the wording of the contract. Many contracts give the seller the right to start foreclosure or forfeiture proceedings and the buyer could lose the property. But with some extra preparation at the time the contract is drawn up, this problem can be eased a bit. The following provision deals with this.

Extension Provision: This escape clause gives the buyer extra time to refinance the home or to sell it to a new buyer who can obtain a loan. There are many ways to word an extension provision to the satisfaction of both the buyer and seller, but in general, it provides a contract extension of 6 months, a year, or more, if the buyer has been unable to refinance. There may be an increase in interest rate and monthly payments during the extension, in order to encourage the buyer to keep trying.

Assumption Provision: Most buyers would love to have the right to let a new buyer assume the contract. That could increase the saleability of the home considerably. Many sellers, however, want to have some say in the matter. They do not want to find themselves locked into a contract with a new buyer who cannot really afford the home. An assumption provision outlines the rules that both parties agree to follow. Will an assumption be permitted, or must the contract be paid off when the home is sold? Will the interest rate remain the same upon assumption? How will the new buyer's credit worthiness be determined? If the answers to these questions are included in the contract, both parties know exactly where they stand.

Determining a Fair Rate of Interest

When institutional interest rates are outrageously high, contracts often are written at a lower-than-market interest rate. That, after all, is one primary purpose of seller financing: to provide affordable financing when it is not available elsewhere. But when market rates are low and money for loans is readily available, sellers often need an incentive to sell on contract. That's when we see interest rates on contracts at or above the institutional rates. You'll often find, too, that contract sales command a higher sales price than a sale involving an outside lender, as compensation for the seller's added risk. Your real estate agent, your attorney and your accountant can give you information to help you determine what is reasonable, based upon other comparable transactions. But the bottom line is this: whatever is acceptable to both buyer and seller, provided it's legal, can be used as the basis for a contract sale. (In the state of Washington be sure to ask your attorney about the provisions of the state's usury law which prohibits unreasonable interest being charged. Oregon no longer has such a law.)

Imputed Interest and the IRS

Sellers may wish to ask the advice of a tax accountant, too, before agreeing to sell a home on contract. The IRS follows an imputed interest rule and it applies to contract sales, as well as other types of seller financing. Generally, it goes like this: if a seller offers financing at an interest rate *lower* than the rate set by the government, the IRS will *impute*, or attribute, a *higher* interest rate to the transaction for tax purposes. For example, if the applicable rate set by IRS is 9% for a long-term contract, and a seller agrees to accept only 7% interest, the seller will be taxed as though he or she actually received 10% interest. The Imputed Interest Rule is complicated enough that sellers are advised to check with an accountant or the IRS before agreeing to a specific interest rate.

Can a Contract Be Used with an Existing Loan

A home with an existing loan may be bought or sold on contract provided there is no due-on-sale clause in the original loan agreement. (A due-on-sale clause requires that the loan be paid in full when the property is sold.) There may also be some conditions set by the lender, which must be followed in the case of a contract sale.

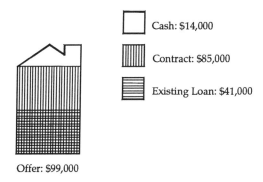

Cash: $14,000

Contract: $85,000

Existing Loan: $41,000

Offer: $99,000

A Contract with an Existing Loan

In the previous example, the Smiths' home is free and clear. There is no underlying loan that might have prevented them from selling their home on contract. Let us suppose instead that there is a loan, with a current balance of $41,000. The chart above shows how the second offer would look.

From the buyer's point of view, nothing has changed. The contract is still in the amount of $85,000, at 10% interest and with monthly payments of $746, principal and interest. The existing loan would remain in the sellers' names and they would continue to make their monthly payments as before. Therefore, the Smiths' net monthly income would be $746, less the amount paid to the original lender.

Lender's Permission to Sell on Contract

If the home being sold has an existing loan, the seller should contact the lender to find out whether or not it may be sold on contract. Most real estate agents routinely obtain loan information in writing from the lender at the time the home is put on the market. They often have form letters that sellers can use to request data. While some institutions will give you an answer over the telephone, many require a letter signed by the borrower (the seller), instructing them to release the information. Be sure to include the loan number for a prompt reply.

When you're asking for permission to sell on contract, it's a good time to inquire about the assumability of the loan also and to notify your lender that you plan to sell your home. Ask for a written confirmation and save it. The buyer as well as the seller should keep a copy. One client of mine agreed to sell his home on contract, but before closing, his lending institution was purchased by another firm with very different policies. Since we had a written confirmation from the first institution, the new lender reluctantly agreed to abide by the old rules. Without it, my client would have been charged an additional $700.

Here Is What You'll Need to Know:

1. May this home be sold on contract?

2. If so, will the interest rate be increased at the time of sale?

3. Must the contract be approved or the buyer qualified by your department?

4. Is the loan assumable? If so, at what interest rate may it be assumed?

5. Will the seller receive a release of liability if the loan is assumed?

6. Must the buyer qualify for an assumption?

7. May the seller carry a second trust deed?

8. What fee do you charge for a contract sale? For an assumption?

9. If the home is sold on contract, may the loan later be assumed?

10. Will the interest rate be increased again?

11. How long will it take you to approve the contract or process an assumption?

12. For how long will this information be valid?

If there is an existing second or third mortgage loan, sellers should contact each lender and ask the same questions.

What if the Answer Is "No"?

Never go behind a lender's back and enter into a contract sale without written approval. Lending institutions have those same extrasensory powers developed by parents of small children. They know everything. Or at least, they'll inevitably find out, and the consequences can be disastrous.

What can happen? If you proceed with the contract sale without the lender's approval, many or most loan documents give the lender the right to call the loan. In other words, the loan must be repaid in full immediately. If you do not have the cash on hand, it may be difficult to scratch up another loan on the spur of the moment. The lender can proceed with foreclosure and the buyer could lose the home.

In spite of these serious consequences, many borrowers have gambled. I have heard these words so often, "This is a big city, the bank'll never find out." Don't count on it! Lenders can and do unearth these clandestine transactions with little apparent effort. When the seller cancels the homeowner's insurance policy and the buyer replaces it, the lending institution is notified. County tax records are a giveaway, as are courthouse files, where the contract is recorded. At the height of the contract mania in the early '80s, when interest rates were extremely high, one loan officer told me that his firm made an effort to spotcheck loan accounts for this very practice.

How "Safe" Are Contract Sales?

There is always some risk in any real estate transaction, but buyers and sellers alike get nervous when there is no lending institution to run the show. Sellers fear that the buyers, who seemed like good solid American citizens at closing, will turn into slovenly deadbeats the following month. Buyers are afraid that they will discover, a week after the contract has been recorded, that the fresh wallpaper in the hall covered a termite jamboree. The time element in a contract sale often exacerbates the problems. Buyers and sellers are locked together in a long-term relationship which gives plenty of time for disagreements to brew.

But it doesn't have to be like that. If you're entering into a contract transaction, take a tip from the institutional lenders. They know how to avoid many of the problems that can crop up and they do it by insisting upon detailed professional reports on both the borrower and the property before making the loan. Would a lending institution take the seller's word that the property is in good condition? Or a buyer's word that he or she is solvent? Are the loan documents blank forms from the office supply store? Not likely!

Is the Buyer Credit-worthy?

Sellers can and should request that the buyers submit a credit information form before the offer is accepted. This form is similar to a loan application form used by a lending institution. A blank may be obtained from your real estate agent or from an office supply store that stocks legal forms. Financial and personal references provided by the buyers should certainly be contacted and assessed.

The preliminary title report, prepared by the company providing title insurance, will indicate any judgments against either buyers or sellers. (Learn more about this in the chapter on Loan Costs and Escrow Closing.) These facts are gathered by the title insurance company from county courthouse records. Be sure to read it and ask your attorney to review it.

Is the Asking Price Reasonable?

The fair value of the home is another question that arises. Lending institutions hire appraisers to evaluate the property before they make a loan. Contract buyers may do the same, if they have doubts about the purchase price. For a single family home, an appraisal of this type will cost around $350. As an alternative, your real estate agent can provide information about recent comparable sales to help determine the fair market value.

Are there any Defects in the Home?

As for the quality and condition of the property itself, buyers should take the time and effort to make a thorough inspection both at the time the offer is made and again, just before closing. It's an excellent idea to hire a professional home inspector to do a complete, whole-house inspection. For a reasonable fee (often $150 to $200), you'll receive a detailed written report of the findings plus valuable peace of mind. Additional in-depth inspections may also be requested if specific problems are suspected: inspections to evaluate the presence of toxic materials, for instance, or plumbing, electrical, or structural defects.

Do You Know the Exact Boundaries of the Property?

Sometimes a boundary survey seems warranted if the property lines are in question. (It's amazing how often fences are in the wrong place.)

Don't be afraid to take the time and effort needed to satisfy any doubts before you closing. Whether you're a buyer or seller, be informed. Rely on professional advice to miminize your risks.

A Buyer and a Property that Are Less than Perfect

With all these precautions and a well-written contract, the risks in a contract sale can easily be kept under control. But that does not mean that a prospective buyer who is a little shaky in the credit department is automatically out of the running. Sellers can be considerably more flexible than an institutional lender and can make exceptions in deserving cases.

Self-employed buyers are a good example. It is often difficult for persons without a regular paycheck to prove their financial worth, to the satisfaction of a lending institution. Lenders have rules that are difficult to bend, especially if the circumstances are unusual. A seller, however, might rely on other factors in order to make a decision and might very well be willing to go where institutional lenders fear to tread. Self-employed buyers, those who have been employed for less than two years, or those with a blemish on their credit history will often find it far easier to buy on contract than to jump institutional hurdles.

Similarly, a home that is not up to snuff by bank standards might be perfectly acceptable to a buyer who understands the problems. For example, a house without a permanent foundation is difficult, if not impossible, to finance conventionally. So is a modest home on an unusually large parcel of property in a residential neighborhood. Both of these would be excellent candidates for contract sales.

Monthly Payment Collection

Buyers and sellers sometimes worry about the handling of the monthly payment. Who calculates the amount that is to be credited toward interest and principal, since those change each month? Many banks, S&Ls and some escrow companies provide a service known as an Escrow Collection Account or a Contract Collection Account. For a set-up fee ($50 to $75) and a small monthly service fee ($5 and up), they will receive the payment from the buyer each month, deposit it and issue a check to the seller. At the end of each year, a written accounting of principal and interest is sent to each party. Arrangements may be made for the payment of an underlying loan, directly from the collection account. This service does not act as a collection agency, pressuring buyers into paying; it simply processes funds as instructed by the contract.

Preparing the Deed

When the last payment has been made, the seller will give the buyer a deed to the property. If the seller has moved to Pago Pago or is on a round-the-world balloon expedition, the deed may not be forthcoming. That is why many buyers and sellers choose to have the deed prepared at closing and held by a neutral party until needed. A Contract Collection Account may offer this service, or an attorney can do so.

Selling a Contract

If a seller needs cash at closing and the buyer's down payment seems all too small, it is possible for the seller to sell the contract for a cash payment. Plans should be made at the time the offer is written, so that terms of the contract will be attractive to a contract buyer. To find out more about this, read the chapter on "Selling a Note or Contract".

Recording the Contract

As in any other real estate transaction, in a contract sale it is customary for an escrow officer to prepare the closing documents, record the contract and disburse the funds. An attorney can handle this aspect of the transaction but many suggest that their clients can save money at this stage, by working with an escrow officer from an independent escrow firm or from a title insurance company. (One exception: in Spokane County, Washington, attorneys or Limited Practice Officers customarily conduct closings.) You'll find more about this in the chapter on Closing Costs and Escrow Closing.

Advantages of a Contract Sale

- Seller and buyer can agree on terms that are attractive to both.

- Buyer does not necessarily have to meet institutional lending qualifying standards.

- Property condition does not have to meet institutional standards, if buyer agrees.

- Seller receives a monthly income, including interest on the equity.

Disadvantages Of A Contract Sale

- Seller does not receive the total equity in cash at closing.

- Seller is absorbing some of the risk that the lender normally takes.

- A poorly written contract can be unpleasant or disastrous for both parties.

17

Other Types of Seller-Financing

Seller-financed Seconds

> *With Seller Seconds, the buyer assumes the seller's existing loan (or obtains a new loan) and gives the seller a note secured by a trust deed for the amount not covered by the down payment and the loan.*

This is a popular method of owner financing in situations where there is an existing loan that is assumable. It is used less frequently with new loans, for reasons I will mention later. To see how it looks in chart form, let's go back to the last example in the chapter on contracts. If you remember, the Smiths received an offer of $99,000 for their home. The buyers had a down payment of $14,000 and asked the Smiths to carry a contract for the balance, $85,000. The existing $41,000 loan would stay in the Smiths' names.

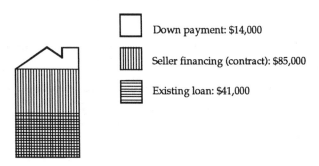

Down payment: $14,000

Seller financing (contract): $85,000

Existing loan: $41,000

A Contract Sale

This same situation could be financed differently. The buyers could assume the existing $41,000 loan, with the lender's permission. (Learn more about assumptions in a later chapter). The down payment would still be $14,000. But instead of a contract in the amount of $85,000, the Smiths would carry a note, secured by a second deed of trust, in the amount of $44,000, the difference between the loan amount and the contract amount, ($85,000 less $41,000).

Other than the down payment, no funds would change hands at closing. The Smiths would receive the $44,000 plus interest later, according to their agreement with the buyers. For instance, the two parties might agree to fully amortized monthly payments over a number of years. Or perhaps they would prefer monthly payments with a balloon payment on a certain date. Interest-only seconds are not uncommon, where the buyer pays no principal at all until the payoff date. No matter what agreement is reached, the buyers are responsible for two separate payments: one to the original lender, the other to the Smiths. The illustration on the next page demonstrates how an assumption plus seller-financed second works:

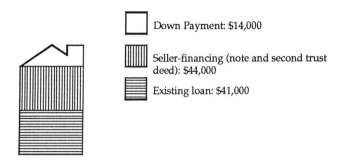

Down Payment: $14,000

Seller-financing (note and second trust deed): $44,000

Existing loan: $41,000

An Assumption Plus Seller-Financed Second

"Notes" and "Trust Deeds" Explained

Notes and trust deeds are not just used in seller financing. They are standard financing documents also used by lending institutions for their real estate loans. A "note," or "promissory note," is a document which describes the debt and the borrower's promise to pay that debt. A buyer will sign the note, but will also give the seller collateral, or security, to back that promise. In real estate, that security is the property itself. A "trust deed," or "deed of trust," is the document that gives the lender (in this case the seller) a legal interest in the property, equal to the amount of the debt. The two documents, the note and the trust deed, go hand in hand.

Why Not a "Second Mortgage"?

A "mortgage" is similar to a trust deed in that it is also security for a note. We often hear the words, "second mortgage." However, most lenders prefer to use the trust deed because foreclosure on a trust deed is a shorter, easier procedure. Mortgages are less frequently used today in the Pacific Northwest, in both institutional as well as seller financing.

Preparation of the Documents

Standard notes and trust deeds are not complicated to draw up. An escrow agent can usually prepare them, at little or no additional charge, while working on all the other closing papers. You may ask for a copy of both in advance if you wish to study them or have your attorney look at them. Sellers, if the note is for a large amount of money or if you have any questions or misgivings, be sure to consult your attorney before closing.

Why This Is a "Second" Trust Deed

The difference between a "first" and a "second" trust deed is not in the documents themselves but in the order in which they are recorded in the county files. The first loan on a home will be the "first mortgage loan" or the "first trust deed loan." A loan or note and trust deed recorded later would be a "second mortgage loan" or "second trust deed." An even later recording would be a "third trust deed," and so on. This is known as the "lien position." If the loan in first position is paid off, then the remaining loans move up a notch. The second trust deed now becomes a first trust deed; the third trust deed becomes a second. The position of the trust deed is important if a foreclosure is necessary. After a foreclosure sale, funds received are used to reimburse the lenders in the order in which the loans were recorded. The first trust deed loan would be paid in full before the holder of the second trust deed receives any money.

In our the example, the Smiths are in second position, whether they carry a contract or a second deed of trust.

Seller-Financed Trust Deeds with a New Loan

Occasionally a seller is asked to carry a second deed of trust on top of a new institutional loan secured by the buyer. Many conventional and government lenders do not allow this; those that do insist that the sum of the payments on both loans be considered in determining whether or not the buyer is qualified. (See the chapter on

Qualifying For A Loan.) Unless the monthly payments on the second are much lower than those on a similar-sized institutional loan, a buyer who is unable to qualify for the full amount owed will not be helped by seller financing.

IRS and Imputed Interest

The Internal Revenue's imputed interest rule applies to all seller-financing, whether it be a contract or a note-and-trust deed. Read the section about imputed interest in the chapter on Contracts and consult your tax accountant or the IRS for current rates.

Contracts vs. Seller-Financed Seconds

Should a seller who is willing to finance the sale of a home sell on contract or allow an assumption with a seller-financed second? Would a buyer be better to assume the loan or to buy on contract? There are no standard answers for these questions. Each situation is different, but by studying the pros and cons of each method, the best solution usually becomes apparent. One deciding factor will be the assumability of the existing loan and the lender's requirements for either an assumption or a contract. Lenders generally, but not always, have more demanding requirements for an assumption, since a seller who carries a contract absorbs some of the risk. Here are other points to mull over as you make a decision. Your attorney may offer suggestions to help you decide.

Advantages of a Seller-Financed Second

- Seller may offer an excellent interest rate and "customized" terms.

- Buyer may find it easier to qualify for this financing than for a new loan, if interest rates on the assumption and second are lower.

- Seller receives an income from the investment, often at an attractive rate of interest.

- Seller is relieved of responsibility of making payments on the underlying loan.

Disadvantages of a Seller-Financed Second

- There is a certain amount of risk in any seller financing.
- The seller does not receive all the equity in cash at closing.

Other Types of Seller Financing

The two kinds of seller financing we have covered are by far the most commonly used. Once in awhile, escrow agents see a variation on the theme, usually under the masterful direction of an attorney. Earlier in this chapter, we dealt with second trust deeds in combination with an assumption or new loan. But a note and trust deed (or a note and mortgage) may be used by a seller in the same way that a lending institution does, as the primary financing vehicle in situations where the property is owned free and clear. In other words, if there is no existing loan on the property, the seller may have the buyer sign a note secured by a trust deed on the home.

Attorneys occasionally recommend the use of a trust deed instead of a land sales contract because of two major differences. One involves the matter of foreclosure or forfeiture procedures if the buyer should default. Another point of difference is the disposition of title to the property. In a land sales contract, the seller usually retains legal title until the final payment has been made. This is not true of a trust deed or mortgage.

Your decision to use a particular form of seller financing should be made with legal counsel. This book can only describe what is commonly done in the Pacific Northwest; your attorney can help you decide what is best for you.

18

Selling a Note or Contract

Seller-financed contracts and notes may be sold at a discounted price, in order to provide cash for the seller.

There never seems to be enough cash to go around. That is particularly true of real estate transactions involving seller-financing. An offer may be perfect in every other respect: top sales price, qualified buyers, agreeable contract terms, and ideal closing date. But if it does not give the seller the cash he or she needs, it will probably be rejected.

The cash problem is a thorny one. Where can you find additional cash, if both buyer and seller have reached their limits? In this book, I have talked about dozens of ways to finance a home, most of which involve new loans. However, there may be reasons why a buyer does not choose new financing. The underlying loan may be assumable at an enticingly low rate, or the home may need some major repairs before it can be financed. In each case, selling a seller-financed note or contract may be just the answer.

How to Sell a Note or Contract

There are companies and individuals who buy contracts and secured notes (notes secured by a trust deed or mortgage) for cash. In financial circles, this is known as "buying paper". It is possible to sell paper for either its full term or for a portion of its full term, for example, selling the contract payments for only the next three years. There is a hitch: selling a note or contract can be expensive. Instead of paying the face value (the actual amount financed), the note or contract is discounted and the seller receives the lower (discounted) amount.

What Investors Look for in a Note

How much the face value will be discounted depends upon many factors, such as the lien position (first, second or third), interest rate, amount of the monthly payment and term, to name a few. Investors (buyers of the notes) use a yield chart to determine what discount to charge, so that their income from the note will yield the desired return on their investment.

Not all investors think alike. Some refuse to buy a note or contract with a balloon payment because of the risk of default. Others think positively with respect to balloons; they consider the early payoff an asset. Some investors want only seasoned notes, those that have been in effect for a few years. Others will buy new notes as readily as old. Many investors specialize in one type of document. For instance, they may buy only trust deed notes and not contracts, or only notes of a specific size.

As a general guideline, the higher the monthly payment and the shorter the term of the note or contract, the higher the price it will bring. Investors like to see hefty payments, amortized over as short a term as possible.

How Much Will Be Discounted?

This is the part that makes sellers nervous. Their first reaction is often a violent one, as they convince themselves that this crazy scheme will never work. Have patience. If the discount cost I am about to mention seems high to you, read on. There are ways to minimize the loss.

You can expect the average second trust deed note or contract to be discounted approximately 20% to 35%. In other words, a seller can expect to receive 65% to 80% of the face value of the second or in the case of a contract, the equity value. But just as each investor looks for different features in a note or contract, so do the discounted prices vary from one investor to another. When I was researching this topic, I gave a sample note to five investors and received five widely differing prices, all within the range mentioned above.

It is sometimes possible to sell for higher than 80% of the face value, if the note or contract includes terms that are particularly endearing to the investor. For this reason, it is a good idea to talk to investors before agreeing to carry a note or contract that you expect to sell at closing or at a later time. Learn what features will make the note more saleable and bring you a higher price.

Here is a situation where buyers and sellers cooperated to make a transaction work:

Case History: The Moores and The Parkers

Julie and Tom Moore wanted to buy the Parkers' home. Jean and Sam Parker needed every penny they could muster for the down payment on their new home, and so they insisted on a cash-out transaction.

"No way!" said the buyers. "We're attracted to your assumable loan as well as your greenhouse and hot tub. We are willing to pay your asking price if you will please carry a note for the $8,000 difference."

The Parkers objected violently. By the time they paid all their closing costs, there would be very little left out of the down payment. They needed more cash. Offer rejected!

Fortunately, they had a real estate agent who wouldn't give up that easily. She suggested that they investigate the possibility of selling a note. The Parkers would agree to carry a note secured by a second deed of trust and would sell that note at closing to an investor. They showed the Moores' offer to several investors, to determine what price they could expect. When Sam Parker heard the results, prices of $4,000 to $5,000 for the $8,000 note, he decided not to move.

"But wait," begged the persistent agent. "Let's try changing the terms of the note, to see if we can improve the price." The agent asked the investors what terms would make them happiest. "Higher interest rate," said one. "Shorter term," said another. Larger payments were important to all.

The trick was to find a combination of all these factors that would bring the best possible price. The resulting note combined an interest rate of 13.5% (up from the original 11%) and payments that increased each month for the first twelve months, on the same principal as a GEM loan. With these increased payments, the $8,000 note would be paid in full (without a balloon) in just under three years. It brought the Parkers, at closing, a price of $6,750, just $1,250 less than face value.

The Parkers were lucky that the buyers were willing and able to cooperate in order to make this work. Not only were the Moores willing to pay the higher interest rate and payments, but they were also able to meet the additional requirements of the investor: It was necessary for them to qualify for the combined payments on both loans and to have a down payment at least 10% of the value of the home. Because the first mortgage loan could be assumed at an excellent rate, Julie and Tom Moore were delighted with their financing package. And the Parkers? Who wouldn't be thrilled to come that close to an all-cash full-price transaction.

Sell Only What You Need

You can reduce the bite of the discount by selling only that portion of the term of the contract needed to produce the desired cash. Another technique could be nick-named the Sell-A-Note/Keep-A-Note idea. This is designed for the seller who does not need to receive cash for the entire amount of the equity. Let's imagine that a seller is asked to carry a $30,000 note, secured by a second trust deed. If the seller were to sell that note, it might bring only $19,000 to $24,000. That means a loss of from $6,000 to $11,000.

But let's suppose that the seller does not actually need that much cash. $10,000 would do nicely, thank you. Instead of selling one large $30,000 note, the seller could divide that equity into two notes, a $13,000 and a $17,000 note, for example, each secured by a separate trust deed. By selling the $13,000 note, the seller could collect the desired $10,000 while losing only $3,000 to discounting. He or she could carry the remaining note, collecting principal and interest each month from the buyer.

In this technique the position of the notes is important. If there is also an underlying loan, one of the notes will be in second position, the other will be a third trust deed note. As explained in the chapter, "Seller-Financed Second Deed of Trust," a third trust deed note is less desirable and potentially more of a risk than a second. Therefore, a third trust deed note may bring a considerably lower price than the range I quoted above. In fact, many investors refuse to buy any note beyond a second. For these reasons, a seller usually sells the second trust deed note and carries the third. Keep in mind, though, in the case of foreclosure, the holder of the third will be third in line for reimbursement.

135

Not Every Note is Saleable

Investors do not buy every note that is offered. They have specific requirements in addition to the terms of the note. Buyers whose credit is poor or who have insufficient income to qualify for all monthly payments will find it difficult to enter into this type of financing. Most investors require a credit report, to be paid for by the buyer. Many investors require a down payment of at least 10% of the home's value; some insist on 20% or 25% down. How that value is determined is up to the individual investor. Many, but not all, want a professional appraisal, paid for by the buyer or seller. This amount is often deducted from the discount fee at closing. Homes that do not pass an institutional lender's rigid scrutiny may still be acceptable to some investors. Standards vary; if the condition of the property is less than perfect, look for an investor willing to overlook the defects.

Where to Find Investors

Although there are dozens of ads in daily newspapers offering to buy notes and contracts, the easiest way to find a reputable investor is through word-of-mouth. Real estate agents can often suggest the names of local companies specializing in small note purchases.

Advantages of Selling a Note or Contract

- Seller receives cash at time of sale.
- May be cheaper for the buyer than a new loan.
- Some investors will consider less-than-perfect property.

Disadvantages of Selling a Note or Contract

- The discount can be costly.
- Investors usually require buyers to qualify for total payments.

Part V
SPECIAL
SITUATIONS

Part V

SPECIAL SITUATIONS

The realm of real estate financing is filled chock-full with special situations. That's what I like about this subject matter: it's varied, always changing, always fascinating to me. But when I see the underwriting guidelines that the major secondary market investors, like Fannie Mae or Freddie Mac, publish, inches thick and overwhelming in their sheer mass and complexity, I wonder how I'll ever be able to distill that information into a palatable form for my books. Of course I can't include it all, nor would you or I want to bother reading some of those obscure facts. Yet there are recurring themes that deserve to be mentioned. Advanced techniques, newfangled twists to a very old game, and nifty ways to leap over hurdles you'll no doubt encounter—all that and more is included in this section that covers Special Situations.

19

Loan Assumptions

In an Assumption, the seller's existing loan is transferred to the buyer, who will then assume responsibility for making the required monthly payments.

Think of a loan assumption as an opportunity to recycle. Take a perfectly good loan, for instance, with a low rate of interest and plenty of years left to run. Why not recycle it to a new buyer, saving all sorts of loan fees and closing costs? Sounds appealing! But unlike other conservation-minded citizens, lenders don't want you to recycle—at least not their loans. In recent years, good assumptions have been increasingly hard to find.

Back in the good old days, in the mid-seventies or so, loans were readily assumable, but who cared? Interest on new loans was cheap, so buyers applied for big, new 30-year financing. Then came the whopper rates of the early eighties, with new loans that were affordable only by the very wealthy (who, in many cases, didn't need them.) The rest of us, when faced with the necessity of buying a home, went after the only cheap money around: the seller's existing loan.

Assumptions became wonderful financing tools when interest rates were unapproachably high. If buyers could step into the sellers' shoes and assume existing loans at, for instance, 7% interest, who would bother applying for new loans at 15%? Almost no one, of course, and therein lay the problem. While this arrangement delighted buyers and sellers, lending institutions were considerably less than enthusiastic. They weren't writing new loans and business was suffering. Moreover, the interest they were collecting on these older loans fell far short of the rate that the lending institutions themselves had to pay to borrow money.

Why There Are So Few Good Assumptions

So the lending industry reacted in several different ways. New, affordable loans (like the ARMs) were created, homeowners with low interest loans were encouraged to pull out their equity via especially enticing refinance offers, and finally, new loans that were issued were not assumable. Since the early '80s, almost all conventional fixed-rate loans have had a due-on-sale clause, preventing assumption. Adjustable-rate loans are often assumable, even today, but they're usually not worth assuming, since the interest rate on these is often considerably higher, or will be adjusted higher, than that on a brand new ARM.

But this elimination of the assumption provision is just one of two reasons why there are very, very few good assumptions to be found today. Inflation has played a part too. Older loans that are technically assumable at an excellent interest rate by now often have loan balances that are ridiculously low, compared to the price of the home. In most parts of the Northwest, housing prices have been leaping upward, leaving loan balances far behind and a gap that's difficult to cash out or finance.

Types Of Assumptions

In general, there are two types of assumptions: one where the seller is still held responsible or liable to a certain degree, the other in which the seller is released from liability. The type used in a transaction depends on the wording of the original loan documents and the lender's current policy. Some lenders offer a choice; most do not.

If the lender requires the new buyer to make formal application and qualify for the loan, that may be an indication that the lender is willing to offer a release of liability. Ask the lender to be certain. An assumption where the lender does not require a formal application and qualification, and where the assumption may be handled entirely by the escrow officer, is probably an assumption without a release of liability.

While the assumption-with-release sounds more appealing to a seller, the alternative, commonly known as a *simple assumption* or a *blind assumption* (because the lender does not need to see the new buyer) is more attractive to a buyer. Blind assumptions are usually less expensive. There is no credit report to pay for and the assumption fee is usually less. The best known simple assumptions are on old FHA and VA loans, although both also offer assumptions-with-release. Because of the low (or no) down payment required on FHA and VA loans, their loan balances are often higher than conventional loans, creating better assumptions years later.

For buyers with a blemish on their credit record or insufficient income to qualify, blind assumptions are the perfect answer, provided the seller is willing to allow the assumption-without-release. As long as the buyer continues to make regular payments to the lender, the seller's liability will never come into play. But in the case of default by the buyer, the seller could be held responsible, to a certain degree. The seller in the following case history was concerned about this.

Case History: Mr. Meyer

One of my clients, a distinguished gentleman named Mr. Meyer, received an offer for his home. The prospective buyer, a young woman, could not qualify for a new loan at the high interest rates available at that time. Instead, she offered to assume Mr. Meyer's existing low-interest loan via simple assumption.

When Mr. Meyer received the assumption information from his lender, he was worried. A simple assumption was certainly permitted, that wasn't the problem. In fact, he was given a choice of either method of assumption. But Mr. Meyer realized that, if he allowed a simple assumption, he would not be released from liability for the loan. He was concerned that the buyer would default and leave him to face the wrath of the lender. Even though this was the first offer Mr. Meyer had received for his home in six months, his first impulse was to reject it.

I suggested that he discuss the matter with his attorney, allowing the lawyer to review the original loan documents. The results were reassuring. According to the bank's assumption department, Mr. Meyer would remain in a position of liability. In a case of default by the buyer, the bank had outlined the steps it would take to recover its loss. First would come the foreclosure and sale, at which the home would go to the highest bidder. But what would happen if the foreclosure sale did not bring in a high enough offer to repay the lender? Mr. Meyer wondered if the bank would require him to pay the difference. (That's known as a *deficiency judgment*.)

The attorney could find nothing in the loan documents that would allow the lender to do this. In fact, disguised in legal jargon was a clause that specifically removed the lender's right to recover a loss in such a way. When this was explained to Mr. Meyer, he accepted the buyer's offer immediately.

Not all loan documents are created equal. Other loan documents may give a lender different rights in the matter of liability. Without a release, a seller may be required to reimburse the bank for a loss after foreclosure if the buyer is unable to pay. An attorney can give you an idea of the risks involved, if any.

Most of today's assumptions require the buyer to make formal application and to qualify for the assumption. To find out the lender's policies, send a letter to the institution, asking the questions outlined in the chapter on Contracts. This will give you a written record of the requirements, costs and time involved.

Assumption of FHA and VA Loans

FHA and VA loans have, in the past, been assumable through either simple assumption or an assumption with a release of liability, according to the seller's preference. In fact both FHA and VA allowed simple assumptions long after the conventional lenders eliminated the practice. However that has changed in recent years. On FHA loans closed between December 1, 1986 and December 15, 1989, the buyers must qualify if the loan is assumed within the first year or the first two years for loans originally made to investors. (Some lenders impose their own two-year rule even on owner-occupied FHA loans.) Both the seller and the buyer remain jointly liable until, after five years, the seller may obtain a release of liability. FHA loans closed after December 15, 1989 are assumable, but not by simple assumption.

VA loans closed before March 1, 1988 may be assumed either by simple assumption, with the seller's permission, or by an assumption requiring the buyer to qualify. VA Loans made after that date are assumable, but simple assumptions are no longer allowed.

Assumption Fees

It is usually less expensive to assume a loan than to obtain a new one. The biggest saving lies in the fee itself. A fee for a new loan is often double the fee for a regular, qualifying assumption, and several times the cost of a simple assumption. Other assumption closing costs are often lower, too. You'll find more information in the chapter on Loan Fees And Closing Costs, but here are some of the major points. Many lenders do not require a new appraisal, since the home was appraised when they made the original loan. For simple assumptions, it is not necessary for the buyer to pay for a credit report. In addition, the buyer saves the cost of a new mortgagee's title insurance policy. The total amount saved by assuming a loan often ranges from a few hundred to well over a thousand dollars.

The Interest Rate Question

Very few loans, except for certain older government loans such as FHA and Federal VA, are assumable at their original interest rate. If the existing rate is low, assumptions usually bring an increase. This change can be a minimal 1% or 2%, or it could be so great that it would discourage anyone from assuming the loan. For example, the rate on some loans changes to the current market rate if the loan is assumed. One lender routinely raises the interest to 1/4 of 1% above the market rate. Even so, for some buyers, an assumption at these rates might still be preferable to a new loan.

Recalculating The Payments

If the interest rate on the loan is increased, the monthly payments will also increase. They must not only be re-calculated at the higher rate but they must be re-amortized over the remaining term of the loan, no longer the original thirty or fifteen years. This shorter term will make the payments higher than they would be for a new loan at the same interest rate. For example, a new $100,000 30-year loan at 10% interest would have amortized monthly payments of $878, while a $100,000 loan at 10% interest and a term of only 23 years would require payments of $927.

How Will You Finance The Gap?

The biggest difficulty most buyers face is not the assumption itself but cashing out the seller's equity. If you have enough cash to pay the seller the difference between the loan balance and sales price, you won't need to read further. Most buyers are not in that position. There is often a hole in the transaction the size of the Grand Canyon, waiting to be bridged in the easiest way possible. An assumption is no bargain unless the secondary financing is also reasonably priced and the buyer is able to qualify (if necessary) for both the assumption and the secondary money.

Earlier in this book, we looked at seller-financed second trust deeds. They are an excellent and commonly-used financing method with an assumption. But what if the seller cannot or will not accept a note? One alternative is to find outside money, possibly a second mortgage from another source. With particularly good assumptions, wrap loans are another solution. You'll find more about these financing ideas in other chapters.

Advantages Of An Assumption

- Lower closing costs and fees, as compared to new financing.

- New buyer may take advantage of a lower-than-market interest rate on some assumptions.

- Buyer may not have to qualify, although this is required on most of today's assumptions.

Disadvantages Of An Assumption

- Excellent assumptions are very difficult to find.

- If the interest rate increases, payments will be re-amortized over the remaining term and will be higher than those on a similar full-term loan.

- Secondary financing is often necessary to bridge the gap.

- A disadvantage to the seller: with some assumptions there is no release of liability.

20

Equity Loans & Purchase Money Seconds

A Second Mortgage (or Trust Second Deed) Loan is a loan that is obtained after the primary financing and so is in "second position". If it is obtained at the time the home is purchased, it is called a "purchase money second"; if it is obtained after you own the home, it is referred to as an "equity loan" or "equity second".

There are several reasons why you might need or want a second mortgage loan. Purchase money seconds, for example, are great gap-fillers. They're often used with assumptions, when there isn't quite enough cash to stretch between the balance on the assumed loan and the purchase price. Then, too, they can be used to give a borrower an extra boost, clear over the Fannie Mae maximum loan limit. Loans above the limit are known as "jumbo" loans; they often have slightly higher interest rates and lower LTVs. A borrower who's just a little over the limit can sometimes do better with a purchase money second and a smaller, more attractive first, instead of hitting the jumbo trail.

A second also comes in handy if you want to make a large lump-sum payment on a fixed-rate loan a short while into the term, yet want to see that payment reflected in subsequently lower monthly payments. Normally fixed-rate loans have hard and fast payment levels; you'd need an ARM to hope for a reflection of the payback in reduced monthly payments. But with a second in the amount of the lump-sum payment, you can use the payment to pay off the second completely and enjoy the low payments on the first alone.

Equity Loans: Bankers' Delight

When the 1986 Tax Reform Act reduced (and finally eliminated) the tax deductibility of interest on personal debt, bankers found a great new way to keep loaning money for all sorts of smaller, miscellaneous purchases. In came the Equity Loan, a slicked-up, renamed version of the old second mortgage loan. Since most home mortgage interest is still deductible, the equity loan offers borrowers a chance to use loans with tax-deductible interest to purchase everything from cars to a college education. (Your accountant can advise you if the interest on the loan you're considering is tax deductible, since there are limits that restrict deductibility.) Seconds have suddenly turned into one of today's best advantages of home ownership. And as anyone who's stepped inside a bank in the last few years knows, equity loans are big business.

Equity Lines of Credit

If you'd like to have an open account that you can dip into for funds any time they're needed, an equity line of credit may appeal to you. There'll be one loan application and one loan approval, and you'll have access to the equity in your home, to be withdrawn in the amounts you wish, at the times you select. You'll pay interest on only the funds you have borrowed to date. Most equity lines are adjustable-rate loans and just like the first-mortgage ARMs covered in an earlier chapter of this book, the interest rate for an equity line is based on an index plus a margin. One significant difference is the repayment schedule. With most equity lines, you 'll pay interest only for the first several years (often 10), then amortized payments over a scheduled period of time. While there is only one loan origination fee, you'll pay an often substantial document preparation fee each time you withdraw funds.

You'll find equity loans and equity lines of credit most noticeably in the consumer loan departments of lending institutions, rather than in the mortgage lending offices, but this is not true in all cases. Purchase money seconds, while virtually identical to equity seconds, are quite often found in with the home mortgage loans. Once you've tracked them to their source, here's what you can expect to find in the matter of terms and conditions.

The Risk is Greater, and Guess Who Pays for it?

Second mortgage loans, whether purchase money loans or equity seconds are a greater risk to the lender than a first mortgage loan. If the borrower defaults and foreclosure becomes necessary, the second mortgagee (the lender) stands second in line behind the lender of the first mortgage financing and behind any legal fees the first mortgagee might incur. At a foreclosure sale, unless the property has appreciated tremendously, there is often little hope that the second mortgagee will get anything but the crumbs of the proceeds.

So to compensate for the added risk, lenders routinely charge the borrower a higher interest rate than that on first mortgage loans-- usually 1/2 of 1% to a full 2% higher. In addition, the term on a second is shorter, usually no more than 15 years and often 10. These two factors produce higher monthly payments on a second mortgage loan, as compared to a first with a lower interest rate and longer term.

149

Balloon Payments are Right at Home Here

Balloon payments are frequently found on seconds. With a balloon, even though the payments are amortized over a longer period of time (15 to 30 years, for example), the loan becomes due and payable at an earlier date (2 to 5 years from closing). Unlike today's first mortgage balloon loans, there are no extension options on these balloons. Do not consider a second that has a balloon unless the amount of the second is small and you are sure you will have funds on hand to pay it off. Never count on refinancing the loan to pay the balloon. You risk losing your home if you're not able to come up with the necessary cash. Instead, choose a loan that is fully amortized, with no balloon.

Other Features You'll Find on Seconds

Seconds may have either fixed or adjustable interest rates. Before making a decision, study the chapters in this book that cover both types of conventional financing and discuss the pros and cons of each with the loan officer. Interest rate and monthly payments may be lower at first with an adjustable rate second but could end up considerably higher before the term is up.

The loan-to-value ratio on seconds is usually much lower than on first mortgages. While first mortgage loans may go as high as 95% LTV, lenders commonly set maximums of 70% to 85% LTV for seconds. That means that the total of the first and second loan amounts may not exceed 70% (or 85%) of the appraised value of the home. Note that private lenders (parents, relatives, etc.) are not bound by these limits. They should, however, check with an accountant or the IRS to learn the tax regulations which apply to this type of financing. You'll find more information about seller seconds in the section of this book on Seller Financing.

Qualifying For a Second

Lending institutions use the same standards to qualify buyers for seconds as for first mortgage loans. However, the monthly payments for both loans are added together and the total is used in the calculations. For example, if a buyer is planning to assume a loan with monthly payments of $525, and is applying for a second with payments of $175, then the sum of the two, $700, will be used for qualifying. Instructions are given in a later chapter, Qualifying For A Loan.

What Will it Cost?

Like standard first-mortgage financing, equity loans or purchase money seconds have closing costs that usually include an appraisal and credit check, a loan fee, mortgagee's title insurance, recording and escrow fees. But because some of these fees are based on the loan amount, the costs for a relatively small second are considerably less than that for a large refinance. As in first mortgage financing, you'll find discount points used to buy down (or buy up) interest rates.

Refinances vs Equity Loans

If extracting cash from your home's equity is your goal, you have two choices. You can refinance the existing first or choose an equity loan or line. (If you're 62 years of age or older, you have a third choice: the reverse annuity mortgage, covered in a later chapter.) Which would be a better choice? There's no universal answer, but here are guidelines for making a choice.

- Consider the interest rate and terms of your first mortgage loan. If the rate is high by today's standards, or if the loan has unattractive features (an adjustable rate, for instance), it may be worth trading in on a whole new (larger) first mortgage loan.

- Consider the amount of cash you need. While you're mulling over the interest rate and terms, take into consideration the size of the "cash-back", especially as it compares to the size of your existing loan. If the cash is a small amount, it may not make sense to choose a major refinance.

- Consider the interest rate, terms, LTVs and payment amounts on both the refinance and the equity loan. Which will suit your need better? Get out a calculator and determine your monthly payments (you can use the amortization chart for short-term loans, too), carrying your calculations ahead several years, especially if you're considering a second with a balloon.

- Consider your closing costs. Many of the financing costs associated with either type of loan are based on a percentage of the loan amount. That automatically makes the refinance more expensive than the equity loan since the refi would be for a larger amount.

Advantages of a Second Mortgage Loan

- Allows the buyer to take advantage of a low interest rate on the first mortgage loan, while still providing necessary cash.

- Equity loans allow homeowners to make personal purchases with loans whose interest is tax deductible.

Disadvantages of a Second Mortgage

- Interest rate is higher than for a first mortgage loan.

- Term of the loan is shorter.

- Because of these, payments are higher, possibly making it more difficult to qualify for financing.

- Loan-to-value ratio is lower than on a first mortgage loan.

21

Refinances

There are many reasons for refinancing a home. Some owners can find a better use for the cash that is currently tied up as equity. Others are tired of paying higher interest rates than those currently available. Many owners have a balloon payment due on a loan contract, and must either refinance or sell. Still others want to change the type of loan, from an ARM, for instance, to fixed-rate financing.

Approach the idea of refinancing with caution. Like any new loan, a refinance is expensive. The lending institution that provided the first mortgage loan may offer a slightly reduced loan fee for certain refinances. Usually the same closing costs associated with any new loan will be charged for a refinance. Because of this expense, it is usually unwise to refinance a high-interest loan for one with less than a 2% reduction in interest. An exception to this might be a move to a better type of financing in the long run. Consider carefully how long you plan to stay in the home. Calculate the costs versus the savings of the new loan with the help of a loan officer. Be aware, too, of other aspects of the exchange. For example, many older loans had better assumption privileges than new loans. Don't trade your home's future saleability for questionable benefits.

An Equity Loan May Be A Good Alternative

If your goal is to obtain cash for your equity, give serious thought to a second mortgage loan, otherwise known as an equity loan. This is especially true if your interest rate is attractively low by today's standards. Depending upon the rates of the existing and new loans, a second may be a less expensive alternative to a whole new first mortgage loan. It's true you'll pay a higher interest rate for a second mortgage loan, as compared to a new first mortgage refinance, but you'll save money in closing costs. Be sure to study the chapter on equity loans to help you evaluate that option.

Rules of Thumb for Refinances

New loans come in all shapes and sizes; refinances are no exception. In general, you can expect to find certain features and requirements to be typical of many refinances. For instance, most conventional lenders have differing LTV standards, depending upon whether you are refinancing to obtain cash for part of your equity, or if you are simply replacing your existing financing with a new loan of a similar amount. In the first case, where you'd like to pocket cash when you refinance your home, you'll be restricted to an LTV of about 75%. For example, if your home is appraised at $100,000 and your loan balance is $60,000, can expect to refinance it up to $75,000, with cash back of $15,000 (less closing costs).

On the other hand, if you aren't asking for cash out of the transaction, your lender can afford to be generous. You'll usually be able to refinance as high as 90% LTV. For instance, if your home is appraised at $100,000 and you're suffering with a $90,000 adjustable-rate loan that keeps scaling even higher peaks at every adjustment, many lenders would be happy to refinance up to $90,000 (90% LTV) provided you will not be receiving any cash at closing. On a second home—a vacation home, perhaps—you'll frequently be limited to a 70% LTV for a no-cash-out refinance and you'll have difficulty in today's lending circles finding a lender willing to make a cash-out loan to refinance a second home.

Closing Costs When You Refinance

As I mentioned earlier, closing costs are very much the same for refinances as for purchase money financing. You'll still need to pay for an appraisal and credit report, plus loan fees and perhaps discount points, mortgage insurance (if required), title insurance for the lender, escrow and recording fees. It is often possible to finance the closing costs on your refinance, as long as the total amount financed doesn't exceed the LTV ratios set by your lender.

Refinancing With An FHA Loan

Both FHA and VA loans are available for refinances, with differing requirements. On FHA loans, HUD will allow up to 85% LTV (including closing costs) if cash is to be taken out, and a higher (unspecified) LTV if the loan is simply to pay off existing loans against the property. In fact, on this second type, with no cash out, HUD has a "streamline refinance" option that allows both owner-occupant and investor borrowers to skip the new appraisal if the closing costs are to be paid in cash. One drawback to an FHA refinance, though, is that omnipresent mortgage insurance. If your refinance is for less than an 80% LTV, you'd do better with a conventional loan, where mortgage insurance may not be required.

There are a few other FHA requirements which may present hurdles to some would-be borrowers. If you bought your home within the past year or purchased it at any time on contract, your refinance amount will be limited to your original acquisition cost, even if that figure is far less than the 85% LTV normally allowed. And don't hope to cash in on the equity tied up in your secondary residence; a cash-out FHA refinance is available only for the primary residence of an owner-occupant borrower. FHA refinances are available from the same institutional lenders who offer new FHA loans. See the chapter on FHA loans for details on finding a lender near you.

VA Refinances

VA also offers a refinance program and "cash out" is now permitted. The loans may also be used to replace existing financing on owner-occupied property. While cash-out refinance loans will be limited to 90% of the appraised value plus the funding fee, some no-cash-back refinances are allowed an exception to the 90% limit. These may be funded up to the lesser of the VA reasonable value or the outstanding balance on the loan to be replaced. Closing costs and discount points may be financed. For manufactured homes, only those with existing VA loans may be refinanced.

Avoid Refinancing By Pre-Planning

Whenever you buy a home, plan ahead. If at all possible, choose permanent financing that will not need to be replaced. Sometimes, though, a refinance is unavoidable. If so, take the time to shop around for the best loan possible. By all means contact the lender who holds the underlying mortgage, but don't stop there. Get a second opinion, then several more, before making your decision.

Advantages of Refinancing

- Change to a more attractive, economical or stable loan.
- Receive cash for part of your equity.

Disadvantages of Refinancing

- The cost to refinance is considerable.

22

Reverse Annuity Mortgages

The Reverse Annuity Mortgage Loan allows homeowners 62 years of age or older to convert the equity in their home to a cash payment or monthly income from the lender. It differs from an equity loan in that no repayment is required until the home is vacated or sold. Also known as a Home Equity Conversion Mortgage (HECM).

It does sound far too good to be true, doesn't it? After decades of monthly mortgage loan payments to the lender, you get to sit back and let the lender send *you* monthly checks! Well, sceptics, this program is one of those rare exceptions in real estate. It not only sounds appealing, but it's also a well-planned and tested program that certainly meets a need.

Homeowners are perhaps the first to recognize that real estate is not a liquid investment. By the age of 62, plenty of owners are living in homes that are free and clear, or very nearly so. Thousands of dollars worth of equity are tied up in the property, while the owners have had no way to convert all or part of it to cash, short of selling the home. They may be sitting on a gold mine, yet not have the financial resources to qualify for an equity loan. After all, equity loans have to be repaid, and require a sufficient and stable income to satisfy lending requirements.

Now the U.S. Department of Housing and Urban Development (HUD) has created a reverse annuity program that allows older persons who own homes with little or no existing mortgage debt to receive either monthly payments or a lump-sum cash payment as a loan against the equity their home. No repayment to the lender is necessary as long as the owner continues to live in the home as a principal residence. When the home is sold or the owner vacates it, then the amount of cash that the owner has received, plus interest that has accrued, becomes due and payable. At that time the loan must be repaid in full, usually through the sale of the home. If the value of the home is far greater than the principal and interest amount at the time it is sold, the owner (or the owner's estate) will retain the balance. If, on the other hand, the value of the property has fallen to a level below the total owed in principal and interest, the owner (or the estate) will owe the lender no more than the value of the property. Any loss to the lender will be covered by FHA insurance.

This is a new program, introduced in May 1991, after a sample test run earlier. Reverse annuity mortgages are beginning to make an appearance in both Washington and Oregon, though it may be difficult to locate a lender, since so few as yet are offering the program. The regional HUD offices in Seattle, Spokane and Portland can supply the names of lending institutions handling HECMs; see the chapter on FHA Loans for the address and phone number of the HUD office serving your area.

How Much Can You Borrow?

The maximum loan amount and the payments received by the borrower are based on a formula that combines several factors: the age of the borrower (or the younger borrower in the case of a couple), the interest rate, and a figure known as the "maximum claim amount." The maximum claim amount is either the appraised value of the home, or the maximum 203(b) loan amount for an FHA single-family residence, whichever is less. (You'll find a table of 203(b) loan information in the chapter on FHA Loans earlier in this book.) The age of the borrower also determines the size of payment. The older the borrower, the larger the payments he or she will receive. The amount of the payments will also depend upon the payment plan chosen by the buyer. There are five different plans, which give the homeowner an option of specifying a particular term, or time period, during which payments will be made. Borrowers can instead request a tenure plan, which will offer them payments as long as they occupy the home as their principal residence. A line of credit plan is available which allows owners to withdraw funds as needed, and there are also combination plans, adding a line of credit to either the term or tenure options. Since there are a number of choices to be made, often by borrowers who haven't applied for a loan in many years, HUD requires that applicants attend a one-time counseling session that will explain both the HECM program and other alternatives.

Fees and Closing Costs

The fees charged are quite similar to those on a standard loan. They include: an appraisal fee, loan origination fee, mortgage insurance premium, recording and escrow fees, plus a monthly servicing fee. Most or all of these need not be paid in cash; some may be financed with the loan, while others will be added to the loan balance as they are incurred.

Advantages of a Reverse Annuity Mortgage

- Older homeowners can afford to remain in their homes.

- It's an excellent and affordable way to cash in on the equity in a home.

- The loan need not be repaid until the home is sold or vacated.

- The borrower does not need to qualify for the loan.

Disadvantages of a Reverse Annuity Mortgage

- In most cases, the home must be sold to pay off the loan (unless other funds are available.)

23

Sweat Equity

> *Sweat Equity is equity that is created through improvements made to the property by the purchaser. The value of these improvements may be considered part of the buyer's down payment.*

It sounds very simple, in fact, deceptively so. Take one "fixer-upper," a home that needs substantial repair in order to qualify for financing. Add a buyer who is willing and able to tackle the job. The result: an ideal situation for sweat equity. (Did I say "ideal"? Most loan officers and real estate agents feel that the words *ideal* and *sweat equity* are mutually incompatible. Perhaps it would be better named,"Blood, Sweat and Tears Equity.")

When it's Good, it's Very, Very Good...

There are plenty of homes on the market that are in too poor a condition to be financed. Institutional and government lenders are very particular about the properties in which they invest. It would be utter foolishness to issue a 30-year loan for a home that will be sagging at the seams in five years. That leaves many sellers in a difficult spot. They could, of course, make the necessary repairs, but only if they have the time, skill or money. The less-than-perfect home may be sold on contract, of course, but if the seller is hoping to sell the contract to generate cash, that may not be possible. Paper is not easily saleable when the property is in need of repair.

There is another alternative: the buyers may be willing to pay for or make the necessary repairs, with the value of the repair work credited to them at closing as all or part of their down payment. If the work is actually done by the buyers themselves, this is known as *sweat equity*. Sweat Equity can work very well with seller financing. Buyers and sellers have the freedom to structure a sweat equity agreement that suits their needs perfectly. But it's also possible to use sweat equity with institutional financing.

But When it's Bad...

Since problems cling to sweat equity cases like burrs to a dog, most lenders groan at the mere mention of the words. The difficulties lie in determining what work is to be done, who is to provide the materials and what the value of the sweat equity will be. It may sound straightforward and foolproof at the outset, but as soon as the buyer uncovers some unexpected structural damage or a bad case of hidden dryrot, the fireworks begin.

There's another problem, too. Watch out, buyers! You're pouring time, energy and sometimes your own money into a home that's not yet yours. What happens if the deal falls through before closing? You've been very generous with your efforts and you've left the seller with a much-improved property. Are you entitled to be reimbursed if you are prevented from closing? You'll want to pay close attention to the recommendations mentioned in this chapter.

Work that Will "Count" as Sweat Equity

A buyer may want to put in a brand new kitchen, complete with tile counters, a greenhouse window and lighted ceiling. Total cost: $4,000 in materials, $8,000 worth of labor by the buyer. The seller says, "Fine with me! That $12,000 can be your down payment." In a case of seller-financing, if both buyer and seller are in agreement, that provision is quite acceptable.

But if a new institutional loan is required, the lender may not agree. Lenders usually allow as sweat equity only those repairs deemed necessary for financing. The buyer in the example above might finish the kitchen, with the seller's blessing, then find that the lender will not allow it to "count" as part of the down payment, since a chic, new kitchen is not considered a necessity. The buyer could then be forced to come up with a cash down payment. If this is not possible, he or she may not be able to get financing. The seller would have a spectacular kitchen and the poor buyer could lose the time and money invested.

To avoid this problem, most lenders insist that loan application be made and an appraisal be completed before any work has begun. The appraiser will determine exactly what needs to be done in order to obtain financing and it is this list of repairs only that will "count" as sweat equity. After the loan has been approved by the lender, subject to the repairs being made, of course, the buyer may start work on the property.

When the work has been completed, the loan officer will ask the appraiser to re-inspect the property. The fee for this inspection is usually $45 to $75, but varies from lender to lender. If the repairs are satisfactory, the closing may take place. If more work is required, another re-inspection and fee will be necessary.

Determining the Value of the Sweat Equity

A buyer may feel that his or her labor is worth a certain figure, but most lenders want proof. Many require three estimates of labor and materials from professional builders or remodelers to establish a fair value for the sweat equity. Some include the cost of materials and labor, others will allow the buyer to count only the value of the labor or materials alone.

You may very likely come up against a requirement that prevents buyers from using sweat equity for the total amount of the down payment. The secondary market investors who buy institutional loans (from lenders) often insist on seeing at least 5% of the appraised value in the borrower's own cash, with the sweat equity used to increase the down payment by an additional 5% or 10%. Currently both Fannie Mae and Freddie Mac, the nation's two major investors, both have that requirement and many smaller investors have adopted that guideline. Still, it's possible to find a lender who will, with caution, accept sweat equity instead of cash for the entire down payment. If this is what you need, call different lending institutions or a mortgage broker until you find one that will accommodate you.

FHA has an additional requirement. Although FHA will consider sweat equity instead of a cash down payment, FHA borrowers must show evidence that they have the necessary skill and time to complete the job in a professional manner.

The Agreement Between Buyer and Seller

Disagreement over money matters is the major source of sweat equity problems. Buyers and sellers who enter into a sweat equity transaction should have a written agreement (included as part of the original sales agreement) that specifies exactly who will pay for what. While it is hard to plan for all the unforeseen difficulties that could occur, the agreement should cover the worst possible scenario. Who will cover the cost of additional repairs that are found to be necessary while the work is in progress? Who will do the extra work? How will this affect the sales price and down payment amount already agreed upon? Will the buyer's investment be repaid if the sellers back out of the deal? If you are planning to enter into a sweat equity agreement—whether you're a buyer or a seller—you would be foolish to do so without legal advice. Ask your attorney to write up your sweat equity agreement, or look over one you've written *before* you sign. As you'll read later in this book, I don't feel it is essential to have an attorney represent you in every real estate transaction, but a sweat equity deal is one situation where I would never consider skimping on legal costs. The odds of a bitter and expensive battle occurring are just too great.

Advantages Of Sweat Equity

- An unfinanceable property can be improved and sold.

- Buyers with little or no cash can work their way to a down payment.

Disadvantages Of Sweat Equity

- Disagreements and unforeseen problems can be disastrous.

- Sweat equity agreements are complicated to write.

- Institutional lenders are reluctant to allow sweat equity.

24

Financing
New Construction

Financing a home that's not yet built is not quite as easy as financing an existing one. New construction is riskier for lenders; most are unwilling to enter into a 30-year commitment based upon a set of plans and the gleam in a prospective owner's eye. The problem is this: until the construction is complete, the home is not much of an asset. If the borrower should default, the lender may be left with nothing but a half-finished basement—and that could be very difficult to sell at a foreclosure sale. Additional concerns about the qualify of construction compound the risk. Lenders have only the builder's word that the home will be built in an acceptable manner.

Over the years, a system of safeguards has been adopted to avoid such problems. First, temporary financing, known as the *construction loan*, must be secured to pay for the costs of building the home. This construction financing is strictly short-term, with an interest rate that's usually about 2% above the current prime rate. Once construction is complete, a permanent loan, like the institutional and government loans covered in this book, may be obtained. This double financing can mean added cost for the borrower, with two loan closings and a double set of fees.

Many lenders today are offering a special "package deal": both the construction loan and permanent financing are included in one loan, with one closing, one set of fees, but two interest rates. You'll be charged the construction interest rate (often "prime plus two") until the home is completed, then you'll be switched to an amortized schedule at your permanent rate. Look into this option carefully; compare the loan fee and other costs for this combination loan to the total costs of the standard two-step method. Often you'll find that the combination package will save you money in closing costs and an even greater amount of stress.

With the two-loan method, there is another disadvantage: although you can certainly apply for permanent financing when you apply for your construction loan, you won't be able to close on the permanent loan until the home is finished. In fact, most lenders will lock (guarantee) an interest rate on the permanent loan for no more than 60 days. Since houses usually take considerably longer than that to build, the borrower is left to wonder what the interest rate will be, and if it will still be affordable. When interest rates were rapidly rising in the early '80s, many people lost their newly constructed homes through foreclosure because they could not qualify for permanent financing at rates that were suddenly much higher than expected. So if you are considering separate construction and permanent financing, be sure to ask your loan officer if there are safeguards to assure that you'll be able to close on the permanent loan.

How a Construction Loan Works

Construction funds may be borrowed by either the builder or the buyer. Some lenders feel that it is easier (or safer) to loan the money directly to the builder. If the buyer secures the construction loan, the builder usually must also be approved by the lender. In fact, many lending institutions will finance only projects built by a select group of tried-and-true contractors. Others will work with any established builder who can supply adequate credentials and a satisfactory financial picture. It is virtually impossible for buyers who want to act as their own builder to obtain a construction loan, unless they are registered and bonded builders with previous experience.

Construction financing has become far more difficult to obtain in recent years as lending regulations in general have been tightened. Lenders are cautious these days and this shows up clearly in loans like these. I don't know of any large, established lending institutions willing to issue construction financing to a non-professional builder. That would not rule out small, private lenders who advertise that they make riskier loans. Another possibility is this: if you already own a home with substantial equity, you may be able to tap into that resource via an equity loan or a refinance, then use those funds to build. Or use stocks, bonds or other collateral to obtain a personal loan for that purpose. Occasionally a builder will obtain financing with the idea that you'll do some of the work. This "co-building" is frowned on by many lenders (they view it as sweat equity and that's almost a dirty word in lending circles) but it has worked in some cases and may work for you.

When you obtain a construction loan, the funds are not dispersed at closing, but are released in a series of draws, at various stages of construction. This is true of both the separate construction loan and the construction portion of the combination package. With both of these loans, the borrower is usually required to make interest-only payments to the lender until the home is completed and permanent amortized payments begin. With the combination loan, you'll usually be given up to six month to finish construction.

Before releasing funds, lenders often ask for proof that sub-contractors and suppliers have been paid by the builder. Construction liens filed against the property by unpaid claimants can force the property into foreclosure if the owner doesn't step in and pay the amount due, even if the general contractor has already been paid. As an added precaution when construction has been completed, a lender will insist upon waiting for the lien period to lapse before issuing the permanent financing. Buyers who do not wish to wait 75 days will usually be required to pay for an "Early Issue" endorsement on the mortgagee's title insurance policy, to protect the lender against unforeseen liens. This costs from $1.50 to $2.50 per $1,000 of loan amount and is usually available only when the builder is qualified and approved by the title insurance company. In addition, a foundation survey is required for most new construction, to assure the lender that the home to be financed conforms with the designated setback and building lines. This will cost the borrower up to $200. Other loan fees and closing costs are the same for new and existing homes.

New Construction with Government Financing

FHA and VA loans are available for borrower-occupied new homes that meet their specifications, but neither will insure nor guarantee construction loans. Both will, however, issue a commitment for permanent financing before construction begins, so that the buyer, lender and builder know that the loan will be available. Many FHA/VA lenders also offer conventional construction loans and can handle both temporary and permanent financing.

For new homes that have already been built, but are less than 18 months old, FHA and VA loans are readily available for those built by FHA-, VA-, or HOW-approved contractors. Homes built by non-approved contractors may also be financed under certain circumstances.

FmHA offers permanent financing for a new home, but a temporary construction loan must be obtained from another source. The builder must be one approved by FmHA.

25

Financing a Condominium

Condo financing closely resembles that for single family housing: same lenders, similar loans. Ditto for Planned Unit Developments, otherwise known as PUDs. However, there are some differences which you should be aware of before you decide to make an offer on a particular unit. Lenders are cautious when financing condominiums since the success of their investment will depend not only upon the financial strength of the buyer and the condition of the condominium unit itself, but also upon the stability and physical condition of the development as a whole. The exterior maintenance and overall management are in the hands of the condominium association. That increases a lender's risk and the added costs of controlling that risk are passed along to the individual buyers.

This shows up in the matter of down payment requirements. Normally, condo loan LTVs are similar to LTVs for single-family homes, if the owner-occupancy rate is satisfactory to the lender. Statistics show that developments with a high percentage of owners living in the units (as opposed to investors who rent the units) are better maintained and a sounder investment. So, most conventional lenders today want to see at least 75% owner-occupancy before they will finance at maximum LTVs. It may still be possible to obtain conventional financing even if the owner-occupancy rate is lower, but you'll need to come up with at least a 20% to 30% down payment to override the lender's concerns.

If the condominium development has been approved by one of the major secondary market investors (Fannie Mae or Freddie Mac), by HUD or by VA, financing will be easier and faster. Before making a loan on a condominium unit, the bylaws and association regulations must also be checked. This can be expensive for a lender and many are not willing to loan on property that doesn't already meet the secondary market's standards. Lenders who have financed the original construction on some of the other units may be more willing to make loans than lenders who are unfamiliar with this particular project.

Your lender may charge an additional loan processing fee for reviewing the condominium or PUD documents; it's wise to ask what the extra expenses will be. Remember, too, that when you're qualifying for a loan, your condominium or homeowner's association fee must be added to your total housing expense.

Government Financing Is Readily Available

Both FHA and VA loans similar to those for other single family homes are offered for condos. (The same applies to financing from the Oregon Housing Agency and the Washington State Housing Finance Commission, both of which offer FHA-insured loans.) VA likes to see a 75% owner-occcupancy rate, but both VA and FHA will consider lower ratios. The development must be on a VA- or HUD-approved list before a loan can be made.

26

Financing
Manufactured Housing

T oday's manufactured housing is better than ever—
and this is reflected in the financing lenders are willing
to offer. You'll find different types of financing, depending upon the source of the funds and the property to be
financed. Manufactured homes and mobile homes are
listed on the county tax rolls as either "real property" or
"personal property", and while definitions differ from
county to county, many jurisdictions consider manufactured housing to be real property if it's on a permanent
foundation on land owned by the owner of the home. At
the other end of the spectrum, is a mobile home without
a permanent foundation, on a rented lot. To most tax
assessors, that would be considered "personal property."

Let's take a look at four financing categories, based in
part on these definitions:

Conventional Financing: Manufactured homes on land
owned by the borrower (with home and land to be
financed together) are eligible for loans similar to those
for site-built homes. It's interesting to note that a permanent foundation is not necessarily a requirement; many
lenders will allow blocks or runners and tie-downs. You

won't generally find high LTVs for manufactured housing; at least 20% down is the norm, with 30% down required on non-owner occupied homes. Interest rates are comparable to those offered for site-built homes and 30-year or shorter terms are available. When it comes to loan fees and closing costs, you'll find that the similarity continues.

Some lenders, though, offer a loan program that's not usually seen in other home mortgage lending circles, a program that allows a seller to carry secondary financing to boost the ratio above the maximum 80% LTV. For example, the borrower might finance 80% of the purchase price, put down 10% in cash and have the seller carry a second trust deed loan for the remaining 10%. While this is not unheard of in site-built transactions, in manufactured housing, the low LTV's have caused lenders to encourage creative financing of this type.

Government financing: FHA and VA both have loan programs for manufactured housing but the conditions under which loans may be issued are considerably more restrictive than that of conventional lenders. To finance manufactured housing as real property, not only must the lot be included in the financing, but with government loans a permanent foundation is required. Loan terms are limited to a maximum of 25 years.

Non-conforming real property financing: Manufactured homes (with land) that cannot qualify for conventional or government financing may fall into this lending category. Single-wide homes, those built before 1976, or those in poor condition can be financed with a non-conforming loan. Also included here might be a borrower with credit difficulties, or a manufactured home on excessive acreage, where the land-to-improvement ratio exceeds the conventional lenders' standards of 30/70 or 50/50. Loans with terms up to 25 years are available, but the interest rates are often 1.5% to 2% higher than those on conventional financing.

Personal property financing: "Mobiles Only" loans, as they're called, are available at shorter terms and higher interest rates than for conventional loans.

Where to Find Financing

Relatively few home mortgage lenders offer financing for manufactured homes. The loans are out there, but finding them can be difficult. After dozens of unproductive phone calls to lenders, you'll be convinced you're the only person who's even considered financing one. Instead, leave the home mortgage lenders to their rumination of 95% LTVs and go where you're wanted. There are mortgage brokers who specialize in manufactured housing and mobile homes, offering an amazing array of financing to choose from. If you're in a small town or rural area, you may have to head to a large urban area to find a broker, but the trip should be worth your effort. Ask a local manufactured housing dealer or a home mortgage loan officer for suggestions on how to locate a broker nearby.

27

Financing Country Property & Vacation Homes

Have you tried to finance a home and acreage out in the country, only to find that the merest mention of the word "rural" makes most conventional lenders shudder? Many urban lenders have geographical areas within which, exclusively, they make loans. Others shy away from the complexities of rural real estate, with wells and perc tests and riparian rights. While it's often possible to obtain a loan for a country home on about an acre of land, in many cases, you'll run into difficulties if you try to finance a home on a large parcel. Since lenders as a rule do not finance bare land, some lenders will base the value of the loan on just the home and its homesite (the acre of land it sits on), giving no value (and essentially no financing funds) to the remainder of the acreage.

Property that is registered in a farm, timber or open space property tax deferral program fares even worse at the conventional lending office. The deferred tax becomes a lien against the property, one that takes precedence over claims made by a lender in case of foreclosure. As a result, such loans are given a very cool reception by secondary market investors (who buy loans from institutional lenders.)

So how do you finance your dream house in the country, if the cityslicker institutional lenders turn you down and if your income is high enough to exclude you from an FmHA loan? Seller financing is a good choice, provided the seller is willing to act as your lender. Here's another interesting place to loanshop:

Farm Credit Services

> *Farm Credit Services (a descendent of the Federal Land Bank) offers loans for rural residences and farms.*

We used to know this lender as the Federal Land Bank, but mergers with Production Credit Association (a lender of farm operating funds) produced Farm Credit Services, which continues to provide financing for both real estate and farm needs. The Federal Land Bank was established in 1916 with seed money from the Federal Government. That money has long since been repaid and the Land Bank became a thriving conventional lender in rural areas. It is a unique organization for three reasons. First, this is a cooperative, owned by its borrowers, who invest in the bank as a loan requirement. Second, it makes long-term real estate loans and agriculture-related business loans only; it does not offer the other services we expect of a bank, such as checking and savings accounts. Finally, it is limited by law to serving rural areas: small towns, rural subdivisions and farms. Financing funds are obtained from the sale of bonds.

Three Kinds of Loans

Farm Credit offers three types of real estate loans. For Rural Residence loans and Part-time Farm loans, a buyer's down payment or equity must be at least 35% or 40% of the value of the property. For Full-time Farm loans, a smaller down payment, a minimum of 15% of the value, may be allowed. Each situation is judged on an individual basis by the loan officer. Loans are also available for refinancing property.

Each borrower is required to invest 4% of the loan amount in Farm Credit Services stock. This may either be paid in cash or borrowed in addition to the loan. When the loan balance has dwindled so that it is equal to the amount of the investment, the invested cash is used to pay off the loan.

Rural Residence Loans

If the property to be financed is a year-round, owner-occupied home on less than five acres of tillable land in a rural area, it may be a candidate for a Rural Residence Loan. The value of the home plus land may not exceed $100,000. (If it does, it may be eligible for a farm loan, which has no ceiling.) In addition, the home must be in modern condition, with all utilities, dependable water and sewage systems, and a year-round road. Farm Credit Services will finance a home to be constructed, if the borrower has a firm bid from a contractor and a workman-like set of plans. No do-it-yourself projects are acceptable.

In determining whether or not the potential borrower qualifies for the loan, Farm Credit is more conservative than other conventional lenders. For a Rural Residence Loan, the borrower's payment for principal, interest, taxes and insurance may not exceed 25% of the gross family income. Many other lenders use 28%. On the Second Ratio, Farm Credit loan officers use a figure of 35%, rather than the conventional 36%, although there may be some flexibility in the Second Ratio.

Farm Loans

Farm Loans are for property that produces an agricultural income. This is how they differ from Rural Residential Loans. Part-time Farms need not be wholly self-supporting, but must show farm income that reduces the cost of ownership. These loans are for borrowers who have other income, such as a regular job, in addition to their profits from farming. There is no limit on the value of the property as there is for a Rural Residence Loan. Refinancing and new construction funds are available. Full-time farm loans are actually business loans, with emphasis placed on the agricultural expertise and business plan of the borrower.

Where To Apply

Loan application must be made at a Farm Credit Services branch serving the particular county in which the property is located. There are forty branch offices throughout Oregon and Washington, so check the telephone directory for the number of the nearest branch. For further information, contact the head office:

> Northwest Farm Credit Services, A.C.A.
> West 601 First Avenue
> Drawer TAF-C4
> Spokane, Washington 99220-4004
> (509) 838-9300

Financing a Vacation Home

Vacation homes, as second homes, are financed with loans similar to those for primary residences. There are some exceptions that are worth noting. For example, high LTVs are rare, if not impossible to find. Most lenders will require a down payment of at least at least 20%. You'll also have to prove to the lender that you have sufficient cash reserves (cash left over after closing) to afford a second home; the reserve requirements are usually higher than those on a primary residence. When you qualify for a vacation home loan, the loan payments on both residences will be used to determine your qualifying ratios. In the aftermath of tighter lending regulation, vacation home financing is still readily available, just a little harder to get. FHA loans are no longer available for vacation property. Likewise, VA loans are not available for second homes.

28

Buying With No Money Down

Turn on late-night television and you'll hear the tempting promises of great and instant wealth through real estate. "You, too," croon the gurus, "can go out tomorrow and, in just five short hours, buy a piece of property with not one cent for down payment." Can it really be done? And more importantly, can it be done without investing in the high-cost instruction materials offered through these television seminars?

The answer to both questions is yes. Buying a home with no money down is entirely possible. In this chapter, we'll discuss some of the basic techniques for accomplishing this. On your own or with the help of a competent real estate agent, you should be able to enter into an agreement to buy a home without spending a dollar. But before you leap at the opportunity, consider the cautionary note sounded here. Sometimes a no-money-down transaction will be more of a liability than an asset. Read this chapter carefully, then decide whether or not you want to proceed.

If You Are a Veteran . . .

First let's clear the slate by looking at two special-interest groups that may buy with no money down: veterans and low-income borrowers.

If you are a veteran who is qualified for a Federal VA loan, you are in a fortunate position. 100% LTV financing is widely available for homes up to $184,000. By asking the seller to pay your closing costs, you can buy a home with no cash outlay. True, you must find a seller who is willing to foot the bill for the extra costs plus the required discount points and seller's closing costs, but some are willing to do so, in order to receive cash at closing for the remaining equity.

If You Are a Low-Income Borrower ...

Farmers Home Administration loans are also available up to 100% LTV, for low-income borrowers who want to buy a modest home in a designated rural area. Refer back to the FmHA chapter for more information about this type of financing.

Other 100% LTV Financing

The rest of the population will not have 100% LTV financing offered on a silver platter. Lending institutions and other government lenders require some cash as down payment. Sellers who are willing to carry a contract or second have no such limitations, although they may find it necessary or prudent to ask for a cash investment from the borrower. If you are a prospective buyer, without sufficient cash to satisfy the conventional lenders, your best chance (other than the two loans mentioned above) of financing a home is through a land sales contract or simple assumption plus seller-financed second.

Clues to a Likely Prospect

When you put in an offer to buy a property with no down payment, you will run into an immediate problem: Almost everyone loves the sound of cold, hard cash. Most sellers would prefer to wait until hell freezes over rather than transfer the property to a buyer with no down payment. Overcoming an owner's objections will be your greatest hurdle. There are certain inescapable closing costs for any transaction (see chapter on Loan Fees and Closing Costs), and you will have to find a seller who is willing and able to pay them. Here are some promising signs to look for when you are house-hunting:

- property that has been on the market for a long time
- a vacant home
- surplus property (an investment property, an extra home as the result of a marriage, etc.)
- a home with an obvious, but repairable flaw, such as peeling paint
- advertisements that use the words "owner desperate," "must sell," or "anxious"
- advertisements promising that the owner will pay all the closing costs
- property with no existing loan, or one that will permit a contract sale or assumption plus owner-financed second with no strings attached

A seller who has no other prospective buyers in sight and who can afford to sell with no money down may accept a reasonable offer. A top sales price and a high interest rate on the offer should produce even better results. Sellers who have other alternatives, however, may be hesitant and may need to be convinced that this offer is a financial benefit. You or your real estate agent can pull together figures to illustrate the advantages. Stress, for example, that this offer will bring:

- an excellent interest return on the seller's equity
- a steady income over the term of the contract or second
- an immediate sale
- immediate relief from tax, insurance and existing loan payments
- immediate relief from maintenance and repair expense

Try to mold your offer to the seller's needs. The one thing you cannot provide is cash at closing, but other points may also be important, such as the overall sales price, the closing date, the interest rate, the size of the monthly payments, the term of the contract, and even your willingness to let the seller have all the draperies or the rose bushes. By agreeing with the seller in some areas, you may win the issue that is most important to you, a no-money-down transaction.

Here are some techniques that are sometimes used to make a no-down-payment offer more attractive to a hesitant seller:

Lump-Sum Payments

You do not have cash for the seller at closing, but could you *build* a down payment over the early years of the loan? Additional lump-sum payments ($250, $1,000, or whatever you can afford) can be made at pre-arranged intervals (every 3 months, 6 months, year, etc.). This would give the seller extra cash and would build up your equity.

Sweat Equity

Although sweat equity was discussed in an earlier chapter, it deserves to be mentioned in a no-money-down context. Institutional lenders are reluctant to accept sweat equity in place of the entire down payment; most require at least a small cash contribution. But sellers are under no such constraint. Sweat equity can work beautifully here for two reasons: first, a home is sold that might otherwise linger on the market, and second, the value of the home is increased after the repairs have been made. This will give the seller an opportunity to sell the note, or you, the buyer, may now have sufficient equity to refinance the home.

Shared Appreciation

Shared appreciation is a technique favored by many of the television seminar instructors. Here is how it works: For a no-money-down transaction, the seller agrees to forego a cash down payment, in exchange for a share of the appreciation (profit) when the home is sold or refinanced on a certain, agreed-upon date. In other words, if a home with a purchase price of $100,000 today is worth $150,000 four years later, the seller would be entitled to a percentage of that $150,000. Obviously this technique works best when market values are poised and ready to rise, but there are side benefits which can be attractive. This will be discussed in the section on Equity Participation below.

Because of the complexity of a shared appreciation transaction, it's wise to consult both a tax accountant and an attorney to give professional advice and to prepare the necessary documents

Refinance with Assumption and Owner Second

Don't waste much time trying to make this technique work, even if you hear it touted on television. It is not easy to accomplish in these days of tighter lending requirements. Here the seller refinances the home before the sale, allowing the buyer to assume the loan at closing. This could be done with a first- or second-mortgage loan. But be aware that few new loans today are assumable and many that are (ARMs, for instance, and many government loans) have stringent rules concerning assumptions and the financial strength of the new buyer. Many loans cannot be assumed immediately and virtually all of today's loans require the new buyer to qualify. Lenders will most certainly refuse to let a buyer with no cash investment assume the loan. To solve this difficulty, the following technique was invented.

Equity Participation (Equity Sharing)

IRS will permit only those persons who hold title to a piece of property to claim the tax benefits derived from that parcel. There are times when a seller would find it advantageous to share those benefits, in exchange for accepting a no-cash offer. (Note: Recent tax changes may reduce the desirability of this technique for you. Consult a tax accountant before trying it.)

The owner of a piece of property may, instead of actually selling the home, remain in title with the new buyer. The two would jointly refinance the property using the original owner's equity. This does not mean that both parties must live in the home, although for high LTV loans especially, many lenders insist that the co-borrower also be an occupant. It is still possible to find financing that allows one co-owner to be an occupant-borrower, the other a non-occupant borrower (usually the original owner).

The advantage to the buyer is that this is a no-money-down transaction (some closing costs may even be financed). He or she must qualify for only a portion of the loan since the other owner will qualify for the remaining percentage. To the original owner's benefit is the tax advantage of property ownership (subject to change) and the possibility of receiving cash for some of the equity at the time of refinance (although many lenders will refinance only up to 70% LTV with cash out. Equity participation works best when the original owner had substantial equity.

Equity participation involves an agreement between the two parties, as well as the joint financing agreement with the lender. As such, it is a complicated technique that should be used only with competent legal and tax advice.

Why a No-Money-Down Transaction May Not Be Desirable

Most sellers want a straightforward sale with plenty of cash. And when the real estate market is lively, most of them can easily get it. Therefore, the buyer or the real estate agent may have a tough selling job, convincing the owner that the offer is an attractive one, albeit unusual.

If the home is in good condition and is well-priced, a no-money-down offer is at a disadvantage. The best properties will be sold via cash, new loans, or seller financing that includes a down payment. Buyers without cash for a down payment will have a very limited choice on the housing market and will often have to pay top price for the privilege of a no-money-down transaction. With the exception of VA and FmHA buyers, the no-money-downers will usually be left with the dregs, those properties that have serious problems or have not been sold after months on the market. While there are exceptions, this is generally the case.

There is another factor to keep in mind: A 100% LTV loan has higher monthly payments than, for instance, a 90% or 95% LTV loan at the same interest rate. For 30-year financing at 10% interest, on a home worth $100,000, the amortized monthly payments would be approximately $878 for a 100% LTV loan, $834 with a 5% down payment and $790 with 10% down. The difference in payment amount can push a buyer out of the financial comfort zone.

If you are a prospective buyer, consider whether or not you want to buy under these conditions. It is often a better idea to wait until you have saved a small down payment; your range of choice will improve dramatically, and your monthly payments will be lower. Once you have a cash down payment, there are usually sellers who are willing to pay your buyer's closing costs in order to be cashed out by a new loan. No-money-down is certainly possible, but the results may not be as desirable as the television seminars would lead us to believe.

Part VI
OBTAINING
A LOAN

Part VI

OBTAINING A LOAN

T he technique of determining whether or not you are able to afford a loan–at least in the eyes of your lender–is known as "qualifying". It's a simple procedure and you won't need a graduate degree in mathmatics to master it. The methods you'll find here are the same ones used by loan officers to assess your borrowing capability, no matter what type of financing you've decided to pursue.

While it's illuminating to work through the qualification process, and tempting to rush out to buy or refinance a home now you know that you do indeed qualify for a loan, I encourage you to keep on reading right to the end. In chapter 31, you'll find some vital pieces of information: the closing costs that will inevitably be charged, no matter how you finance. For many borrowers, they're an eye-opener; they can exceed many a down payment. So it's far better to be prepared well in advance for what you're likely to encounter at the closing table.

Here's a tip for prospective homebuyers who are faced with a real estate boom, a wild and crazy seller's market. You can give your offer additional clout at the bargaining table by asking your lender to *pre-approve* your loan. Before you've even found the home you'd like to buy, many lenders will run all the necessary credit checks and employment verifications and will give you a firm commitment for the maximum loan you're qualified to receive, provided that the home you want to buy is acceptable to the lender. (The home will be appraised after your offer's been accepted.) Think of the advantages to the sellers if they decide to accept your offer: you're a sure-fire bet, with financing in hand. There's no need to take the home off the market and wait to see if you'll be approved. That should make your offer especially appealing in the negotiating process.

29

Qualifying
For a Loan

If you've been toying with the idea of buying the lumber baron's mansion on the hill overlooking town, study this chapter before you fall irrevocably in love with the place. It's a good idea to know where you stand in the matter of financing, in order to eliminate the risk of a broken heart.

Just how large a loan can you expect to get from a lender, considering your particular income and debts? Is the lumber baron's mansion within your financing capabilities, or should you be shopping for a three-bedroom ranch? To find the answers to these questions, "qualify" yourself, using the instructions that follow. Or ask a loan officer or real estate agent to do the calculations for you. (Please note that real estate agents and most loan officers work on a commission basis rather on a salary. In return, they would like to have an opportunity to do business with you when you are ready to buy, sell or borrow.)

The methods used to qualify borrowers vary with different types of loans. While there is some standardization among conventional lenders, governmental agencies often have their own special computation techniques. The important thing for a prospective borrower to do first, however, is to get a general idea of his or her financial comfort zone. That is the purpose of the Ballpark Estimate I've included in this chapter. By following the instructions, you'll have a rough idea of the size of loan you could receive. Although the directions are based on conventional qualifying methods, the results will be reasonably close to government loan standards to give an approximate amount there, too. That will help you decide whether to inspect the lumber baron's mansion or to cross it off your list.

Once you have narrowed your sights to a particular home, loan type and amount, you'll want to know if you can qualify for that specific loan. Later in this chapter, you will find worksheets designed for this purpose, using qualification methods for conventional, FHA and VA financing. Use the FHA ratios for loans from the Oregon Housing Agency and either FHA or conventional ratios for Washington State Housing Finance Commission loans, depending upon the program selected. For subsidized loans, such as the FmHA program, ask your loan officer to run the necessary calculations.

Calculating the Ballpark Estimate

Before the calculations begin, there is some information you will need to assemble. A quick call to a lending institution (ask for the Mortgage Loan Origination Department) or to a real estate agent should be all that is needed. Your insurance agent can give you the approximate insurance figure you'll need.

What Is The Average Interest Rate On A New Loan?

If you know what type of loan you are interested in, such as a 1-year ARM, then ask for that specific rate. If you are "just looking," ask for an average rate for a fixed-rate 30-year loan and a range of rates for ARMs. Remember too, that some loans have an introductory rate that is different from the note rate. Find out which rate will be used as a basis for qualification.

Will mortgage insurance be required?

If so, what will the monthly premium be? To understand what mortgage insurance is and what it will cost, read the section that deals with it in the chapter on Loan Fees and Closing Costs. If your down payment (or equity, if you are refinancing) is less than 20% of the value of the home, mortgage insurance will probably be required by conventional lenders. While mortgage insurance is required on all FHA loans, it is handled differently. If you are considering FHA financing, be sure to study that chapter first.

What would the property taxes and homeowners insurance be for the type of home you'd like to buy?

Real estate agents and your insurance agent can give you a rough idea of what these annual costs would be for a certain size of home in a particular area.

Now you are ready to qualify yourself. Since most conventional lenders qualify buyers in two steps, known as the *Housing Cost Ratio* and the *Total Debt Ratio*, we will work through both procedures. Both ratios must fall within the acceptable limits in order for the borrower to qualify for the loan.

Rule of Thumb for Conventional Loan Qualification

Many conventional lenders use the following percentages to determine loan eligibility:

- Monthly housing costs (principal, interest, mortgage insurance, property taxes, association dues, plus homeowner's insurance) may not exceed 28% of the borrower's gross monthly income, and in addition,

- Total monthly debts (all of the above plus car payments, other loan payments, credit card expenses, alimony, child support, etc.) may not exceed 36% of the borrower's gross monthly income.

Note these exceptions to the rule of thumb:

- Conventional loans over 90% LTV use 25% and 33%.

- FHA loans use 29% and 41%

Qualification percentages vary somewhat from lender to lender and from loan to loan. For buyers with excellent cash reserves and a strong credit history, standards of the Second Ratio (Total Debt Service Ratio) are often relaxed to 38%. For loans with temporary buydowns, some lenders restrict the Second Ratio to 33%. The percentages quoted here are typical and will give a good overall picture of your financing capabilities.

Now, have paper, pen and a calculator ready, and start computing:

The Ballpark Estimate

Housing Cost Ratio ("First Ratio")

STEP 1: Determine your gross monthly income; that is, your income before taxes are deducted. For example, if you are paid weekly, multiply your weekly gross pay by 52, then divide by 12. For two-week pay periods, multiply by 26 before dividing by 12.

If your income is not in the form of a regular paycheck from an employer, or if part of your income is from bonuses, commissions or interest payments, read 'Is It Considered Income?' later in this chapter. Ditto if you are self-employed or have been employed at your present job less than two years.

STEP 2: Multiply your gross monthly income by .28.

Example: Gross monthly income of $3,000 x .28 = $840. This figure (the $840) is the maximum amount the bank will permit you to pay each month for housing costs (principal, interest, property taxes plus homeowner's insurance.)

STEP 3: From the answer obtained in Step 2, deduct the cost per month of property taxes, homeowner's insurance, association fees, if any, and mortgage insurance premium, if required). If you have been given annual figures, divide by 12 to determine the monthly cost.

Example:

Add together: Property Taxes	$200
Homeowner's Insurance	$50
Mortgage Insurance	$20
	$270
Deduct this from your answer to Step 2:	$840
	-270
	$570

This is the maximum amount you will be permitted to spend on monthly principal and interest payments.

STEP 4: Using the amortization chart in the Appendix at the back of the book, find the factor that is based upon the interest rate on a new loan and the term (length) of the loan.

Example: If the interest rate on a new 30-year loan is 10%, the factor, according to the amortization chart is 8.78. The factor would be the same for any 30-year loan at 10%, whether it has a fixed or adjustable rate.

STEP 5: Divide your answer to Step 3 by the factor in Step 4, then move the decimal point three places to the right.

Example: $570 ÷ 8.78 = 64.92027   ($64,920.27)

This gives you the maximum loan amount you may be qualified to borrow using the Housing Cost Ratio. But this ratio is only half the story! You must now see how you qualify using the Total Debt Service Ratio.

195

BALLPARK ESTIMATE WORKSHEET

HOUSING COST RATIO:

Gross monthly Income..................	$...............
(Multiply by .28)	x .28*

A. Max. allowed for housing costs $...............

Monthly costs of:
Property Taxes.............................	$...............
Homeowner's Insurance...............	$...............
Mortgage Insurance......................	$...............
Association Fees...........................	$...............

B. Total monthly housing costs.... $...............

**C. Max. allowed for monthly
  principal and interest...............** $...............
(Subtract line "B" from line "A")

Loan Data:
Interest Rate...................................	.... %
Term of Loan.................................	.... years

D. Amortization Factor.................   ....
(Use chart in Appendix)

**E. Max. loan amount - Housing
  Cost Ratio....................................** $...............
(Divide line "C" by line "D" and move the
decimal point 3-places to the right)

Line "E" is the maximum loan amount determined by the
Housing Cost Ratio.

* For 95% LTV conventional loans, use 0.25
  For FHA loans, use 0.29

TOTAL DEBT SERVICE RATIO

Gross Monthly Income............... $..............
(Multiply by .36)   x .36 *
F.Max. allowed for housing costs
plus total debts........................... $..............

Total monthly debts:
Property Taxes........................... $.................
Homeowner's Insurance.............. $.................
Mortgage Insurance.................... $.................
Association Fees........................ $.................
Car Payment.............................. $.................
Other Loan Payments.................. $.................
Total Credit Card Payment.......... $.................
Alimony / Child Support.............. $.................
Other monthly payments.............. $.................

G. Total monthly debts.................. $.................

H. Maximum principal and
interest payments...................... $..............
(Subtract Line "G" from line "F")

I. Maximum loan amount - Debt
Service Ratio............................. $..............
(Divide line "H" by line "D" and move the
decimal point 3-places to the right)

Line "I" is the maximum loan amount determined by the Total Debt Service Ratio. Study the instructions preceeding this worksheet to interpret the results of your calculations.

* For 95% LTV Conventional Loans, use 0.33
  For FHA Loans, use 0.41

Total Debt Service Ratio ("Second Ratio")

STEP 1: Multiply your gross monthly income by .36 (or by the percentage for the Total Debt Service Ratio given to you by the loan officer. It will be a number close to .36).

Example: $3,000 x .36 = $1080

This is the total amount the lender will allow you to spend on housing costs (principal, interest, taxes and insurance) plus your regular monthly debts (car payments, other loans, alimony, child support, credit card payments, etc.).

STEP 2: Add up all of these monthly debts except principal and interest, then subtract the total from your answer to Step 1.

Example:

Property Taxes	$200.
Homeowner's Insurance	$50.
Mortgage Insurance	$20.
Car Payment $	225.
Visa	$50.
Total monthly debt service:	$545.
Then subtract:	$1080.
	-545.
	$535.

This is the maximum amount the lender will permit you to spend on monthly principal and interest payments, using the Total Debt Service Ratio.

STEP 3: Divide the answer to Step 2 by the factor you used in Steps 4 and 5 above.

Example: $535 ÷ 8.78 = 60.93394   ($60,933.94)

This is the maximum loan amount you are qualified to borrow on the basis of the Total Debt Service Ratio.

If the two ratios give different results, which is correct?

> *If the maximum loan amount on the First Ratio exceeds that on the Second Ratio, the latter amount will usually be your top borrowing limit.*

You can expect the maximum loan amounts to differ; it would be far more surprising to have a matched set of figures. But which will the lender use to determine how much you can borrow? Here are the guidelines:

Example: In our calculations above, the maximum loan amounts for our borrower were as follows:

First Ratio $64,920.27
Second Ratio $60,933.94

The borrower's total monthly debts are higher than the lender would allow for a $64,920 loan. Therefore, he or she could borrow only $60,933, the amount on the Second Ratio.

> *If the maximum loan amount on the Second Ratio exceeds that of the First Ratio, pat yourself on the back. Your total debts are less than the allowable limit. In this case, the First Ratio percentage may be raised, at the discretion of the lender, to 30% or even 32%, and the First Ratio figure will be used as the maximum loan amount.*

Example: If, in our Second Ratio example above, the borrower had no car loan or monthly Visa payment, the total monthly debt service (excluding mortgage loan payment) would be only $270, instead of $545. After recalculating, we would find that the new maximum loan amount on the Second Ratio is $92,255. An astounding difference! In the case of borrowers with little or no debt, most lenders take this high second ratio figure into consideration when qualifying borrowers. While a loan as high as $92,255 would probably not be permitted since it violates the

First Ratio guidelines, a lender might be willing to bend the 28% rule to allow a 30% or 32% First Ratio. That could allow our borrower a maximum loan amount of $71,000 to $78,000.

Now calculate your own ballpark estimate using the blank worksheet.

Getting Down to Specifics

This estimate will get you into the ballpark, but when you are ready for the last inning of the financing game, you will want specific batting averages. Use the following worksheets when you know the size of loan you need and the particular home you hope to finance.

They will answer the ultimate question, "Can I afford it?", or in other words, "Do I qualify for this loan?" You may have to try various loan programs, at different interest rates or terms, until you find one that fits.

Different worksheets and ratios are included, for different types of financing. The conventional method is a basic one, with a variation on the theme used by FHA. VA uses a different technique. You'll find the worksheets very straightforward and easy to use.

Remember that there are "grey areas" and extenuating circumstances in many financing situations. If your calculations show that you do not qualify for the loan, don't be discouraged. It's impossible in a book this size to list all the determining factors that will make a difference to your particular lender at the moment your application comes up for consideration. However competent loan officers are adept at helping borrowers find hidden assets they had no idea could be used in their favor. Quite often, a loan officer will suggest a small change that will make a significant difference in the loan application.

Is it Considered Income?

When using a qualification worksheet, the question of income arises. What may or may not be considered income? May bonuses, alimony, child support, and interest earned from stocks, bonds or notes be counted in the qualifying ratios? Lenders use the terms "sustained," "stable" or "steady" to define income that is acceptable for this purpose. If an applicant received a $20,000 bonus last year, it will be counted as income only if the bonus has been that large in previous years and is certain to continue.

A man I sold a home to a few years ago, regularly received a $5,000 bonus each December. Just before he applied for the loan, he was promoted to the position of district manager. He was told that he could expect a higher bonus, one between $8,000 and $12,000, depending upon the company's sales. The underwriters refused to allow the bonus to be included as income for two reasons: first, the employer would not sign a letter of guarantee that the bonus would be paid, and second, the applicant was new to his job and could not show a steady string of such bonuses for this work. The irony of the situation was that, had he not accepted the new position, the underwriters might have included his $5,000 bonus as income, since he had consistently earned one for the past several years.

There is no standard guideline for non-salary income. Your loan officer can cite institutional policy, but much will depend upon the underwriters' view of your overall financial picture. Self-employed applicants often have a more difficult time in proving a stable income. For this and other kinds of irregular income, adequate documentation is essential. Be prepared to back up your claims with several years' income tax returns and other evidence of income. In filling out the worksheets, consider only the income that is steady and predictable. Everything else is just frosting: nice if you can use it, but don't count on anything other than plain cake.

CONVENTIONAL & FHA QUALIFICATION WORKSHEET

Loan Amount .... at .... % interest

Applicant's Gross Mo. Income...	$.............
Spouse's Gross Mo. Income.......	$.............
A. Total gross monthly income:	$.............

Monthly housing expense:

Loan Payment (principal & interest; see Appendix)............	$.............
Estimated monthly prop. tax.......	$.............
Estimated monthly homeowner's insurance................................	$.............
Private mortgage insurance premium, if any......................	$.............
Association fees, if any...............	$.............
B. Total monthly housing cost:	$.............

Total monthly debts:

Housing cost (line "B")...............	$.............
Automobile loan payment...........	$.............
Other loan payments..................	$.............
Child support / alimony..............	$.............
Credit card payments..................	$.............
Other monthly obligations...........	$.............
C. Total monthly debt service:	$.............

For this worksheet we will use 28% and 36% for the two ratios. If the particular loan you are applying for has different requirements, use the percentages suggested by your loan officer. Remember that you must qualify for both ratios.

HOUSING COST RATIO: Line "B" must not exceed 28%* of line "A". Line "B" ($) divided by line "A" ($) must equal .28* or less to qualify.

TOTAL DEBT SERVICE RATIO: Line "C" must not exceed 36%** of line "A". Line "C" ($) divided by line "A" ($) must equal .36** or less to qualify.

* Use 25% (0.25) for 95% LTV Conventional Loans or 29% (0.29) for FHA Loans.

** Use 33% (0.33) for 95% LTV Conventional Loans or 41% (0.41) for FHA Loans.

VA QUALIFICATION WORKSHEET

Loan amount at $.................... at .... % interest.

Mortgage payment (P&I), see
   Appendix 1................................ $...............
Estimated monthly property tax....... $...............
Estimated monthly fire insurance..... $...............
Monthly maintenance expense.......... $...............
Monthly heat and utilities................ $...............
A. Total monthly shelter cost........ $...............

Monthly obligations (over 6 months) $...............
Automobile payment........................ $...............
Other loan payments........................ $...............
Credit card payments....................... $...............
Other.. $...............
B. Total monthly debts................... $...............

C. Gross monthly income.............. $...............

Federal income tax (monthly)......... $...............
State income tax (monthly).............. $...............
Social Security (monthly)................ $...............
Other payroll deductions.................. $...............
D. Total deductions......................... $...............

Net take-home pay........................... $...............
   (line "C" minus line "D")
Less monthly shelter costs and
   monthly debts (lines "A" and "B") $...............

E. Balance available....................... $...............

Compare line "E" to the chart below based on family size (vet. + spouse + dependents). Line "E" must be equal to or greater than the chart amount in order to qualify for the loan.

	For loans of $69,999 + below:	For loans of $70,000 + above:
Single vet	$ 409	$ 472
Family of 2	$ 686	$ 791
Family of 3	$ 826	$ 952
Family of 4	$ 930	$1,074
Family of 5	$ 965	$1,113

Your loan officer will check a second way: add the monthly loan payment, property taxes and insurance (PITI) to line "B". Divide your answer by line "C". The answer should be less than .41 to qualify, although VA allows this ratio to be higher if there are strong compensating factors.

30

Loan Processing: From Application to Approval

Most loans are processed by banks, S&Ls, mortgage companies and mortgage brokers. These institutions take applications not only for conventional loans but also for some types of government-backed financing such as FHA, VA, the state first-time buyer programs, and an increasing number of FmHA loans. Not every lending institution handles all types of loans, so be sure to choose one that offers the particular program you have in mind.

How to Choose a 'Good' Lender

One day, a branch manager for a lending institution was on HOUSE CALLS and when I opened the line for calls, she was confronted with a blast of frustrations from would-be buyers and sellers alike. They felt helpless and exasperated in their dealings with other loan officers. Poor communication, or no communication whatsoever, headed the list of complaints by a long shot. Tied into that was what I'll call foot-dragging, a not very aggressive approach to paper processing. Finally, came the charge of overall incompetence, from a surprising number of callers. It probably discouraged a great many of listeners from ever attempting to finance a home!

So how do you find a good loan officer when you need one? To begin with, you'll have a wide choice of lending institutions, banks, savings & loans, and mortgage companies, as well as mortgage brokers, who process loans and channel them to any one of several lending institutions, in your state or across the country. Today, lending institutions are bound by so many governmental regulations and lending restrictions that there's great similarity between them in the mechanics of loan processing. That does not, however, mean that all lending institutions are equal. And to carry it a step further, it should be obvious to students of human nature that not all loan officers are equal in their skill and work habits.

I find that most borrowers are tempted to go where the interest rates seem lowest. That's a foolish idea for a couple of different reasons. First, as you know from reading earlier chapters, in this untamed jungle of mortgage financing, with its discount points and loan costs that multiply like fleas, nobody can begin to guess who has the lowest rates in town. Second, if you, by some clairvoyant power could find the institution with the lowest rates, by the time you've made loan application, the lender across the street may have beat this one by at least a half a percent. What is most important in any transaction is what the listeners on HOUSE CALLS voiced. A conscientious loan officer and a lending institution that processes its loan applications efficiently are worth plenty of consideration. Ask your real estate agent for recommendations; agents work closely with loan officers and know who will do an excellent job.

Why You Can't Argue with a Loan Officer... and Win

I once watched an inexperienced loan officer drown a prospective borrower in a sea of unfamiliar words. The monologue was peppered with unexplained phrases such as "cap rate," "GEM features," and "negative amortization." Then the speaker began extolling the virtues of Fannie Mae, noting with obvious satisfaction that the condominium to be purchased met with her approval. The applicant, by this time, had reached a point of complete exasperation. He jumped up and demanded, "Who the hell is Fannie Mae anyway? And why should she give a damn about my condo?"

Fannie Mae commands respect in lending circles. So do her sidekicks, Ginnie Mae and Freddie Mac. These three, properly named the Federal National Mortgage Association (FNMA), the Government National Mortgage Association (GNMA), and the Federal Home Loan Mortgage Corporation (FHLMC) respectively, buy loans from lending institutions on what is known as the *secondary market*. Although these are the major investors in home mortgage loans, other investors get into the act. Insurance companies, for example, also buy heavily on the secondary market. Since loans are sold in groups, or blocks, worth millions of dollars, the investors are usually large corporations or syndicates of individual investors. Loans are sold on the secondary market to generate cash, which can, in turn, be used to finance other loans. Some lenders "portfolio" (keep) a greater percentage of loans than others, but it is very likely that your loan will be sold to an investor at least once.

Investors Call the Shots

Investors are very fussy when it comes to buying loans. With that money behind them, they can call the shots. Each investor issues a set of guidelines for the loans to be purchased and lenders must follow these to the letter if they hope to sell the loan to that buyer. Lenders are certainly anxious to sell! As one loan officer put it, "The only good loan is a saleable one. An even better loan is one we've already sold."

Because Fannie Mae has immense buying capability, the FNMA guidelines are treated with almost as much reverence as the Ten Commandments. Lenders cannot afford to ignore them. That is why, if Fannie Mae (or another investor) specifically requires mortgage insurance on all loans over 80% LTV, a borrower's tearful plea for no PMI will fall on deaf ears. That, in a nutshell, is why you can't argue with a loan officer, and win.

Non-Conforming Loans

But surely, you say, there is an investor somewhere with a different taste in loans. Yes, that's quite true. Not all guidelines are the same. For example, you'll find some investors willing to purchase "no-doc" or "low-doc" loans today. (These are loans with large down payments but inadequate documentation of income, often from self-employed borrowers.) Fannie Mae and Freddie Mac aren't interested in these, but other investors still buy them. You will find differences, but common sense and good banking practices usually prevail. Investors will not go too far out on a limb and risk buying shaky loans.

One FNMA guideline is commonly ignored by other investors: the maximum loan amount on any loan purchased. Both FNMA and FHLMC have a current limit of $203,150 but this is reviewed each December and increases frequently. (GNMA buys FHA, VA and FmHA loans, all of which have their own limits.) Who finances the $500,000 homes? Other investors fill this need and so lenders are able to offer larger loans, known in the trade as *jumbo loans* (usually at a slightly higher interest rate and lower LTV). These, and any other loans that do not follow Fannie Mae or Freddie Mac guidelines are called "non-conforming" loans. They will still be sold, but to investors who play by different rules.

Who Will Buy My Loan?

When an investor buys your loan, you may not even know it. Your lender may continue to "service" the loan, receiving your monthly payment as usual. Often when the loan is sold the servicing is sold too; one day you'll receive a letter from your old lender plus a letter from the investor instructing you to begin sending your payments to XYZ Bank in upstate New York. You have no control over the sale of your loan; I know of no sure-fire way to avoid it in today's lending circles.

Working with a Mortgage Broker

Mortgage brokers take loan applications and process them for institutional lenders. They do all of the "up front" work—credit check, appraisal, employment verification, etc.—and submit the package to a lending institution for approval. You will not pay an additional fee for this service; the mortgage broker is paid by the lender out of the standard fees charged with a new loan. However, there are two advantages to consider. First, mortgage brokers offer loans from a wide variety of sources, some of which are "wholesale lenders" only (they don't deal directly with borrowers). As a result, you may have access to new and different loans, with different lending requirements. Second, if you fail to get loan approval from one lender, a mortgage broker can often submit your application to another lender, since the appraisal is made in the mortgage broker's name, rather than in the name of the first lender. Your chances of getting a loan from a distant bank are somewhat greater than with a local lender, but now that loans are sold frequently, this is of less importance.

"May We Pick Up the Check on Tuesday?"

Many borrowers are surprised to learn that it takes from four to eight weeks to obtain new financing. The largest portion of that time is spent in verifying the borrower's credit information and in collecting data needed by the underwriters in making a decision. Once the pertinent facts and documents have been assembled, the underwriters need very little time to approve the loan, from several hours to a few days at most.

You can accelerate the process by giving the loan officer a head start on the paperwork. If you arrive at the loan application interview (otherwise known as the 'loan app') with all the necessary information in hand, the processing time for your loan will be considerably shorter, closer to the four- rather than the eight-week mark. For most loan assumptions today the same information and documents will be needed.

Preparing For Loan Application

Here is a checklist to get you ready for your meeting with the loan officer.

LOAN APPLICATION CHECKLIST

I. Your checkbook, to pay for the credit report and appraisal (these must be paid for at loan app.)

II. Information about the home:

> 1. a legible and complete copy of the sales agreement
> 2. a copy of the earnest money check or note
> 3. a 'trio' (from your real estate agent or title insurance company) or other documents showing legal description
> 4. name and phone number of person who can give appraiser access to the home
> 5. for VA loans: copies of heat and utility bills for the past 12 months or signed statement from seller showing costs
>
> (eliminate items 1 and 2 if refinancing)

III. Personal information (for applicant and spouse if both incomes are to be counted or if both will take title to the property):

> 1. current home address and phone number
> 2. previous home address for the past four years
> 3. birth dates
> 4. Social Security numbers
> 5. name and address of current employers
> 6. name and address of previous employers (past two years)
> 7. for veterans' loans (VA, FHA 203(b)2) a copy of your discharge paper (DD214)
> 8. for VA loans: name and address of your nearest living relative

IV. Assets and Liabilities (for applicant and spouse as above):

> 1. current gross salary (before deductions)
> 2. list and amounts of paycheck deductions
> 3. income for the past three years (from all sources)
> 4. if you work on commission: federal income tax returns for the past three years
> 5. if you are (or were) self-employed: federal income tax returns plus profit and loss statements for the past three years (a CPA's signature is often required)

6. record of benefits received, such as social security, disability, veterans' benefits

7. names, addresses and account numbers of all banks, S&Ls, credit unions, etc. where you have a savings or checking account plus the approximate balance of each account

8. names, addresses and account numbers of all your credit cards and credit accounts, plus the balance and monthly payments required on each (this includes everything from Mastercard and Visa, to department store credit cards and your charge account at the local hardware store)

9. names, addresses, account numbers, monthly payments and balance of any current or previous loans, such as other mortgage loans, car loans, student loans, etc.

10. record of any stocks or bonds that you own plus name and address of brokerage firm that can verify holdings

11. proof of any assets such as cash value life insurance or retirement fund

12. if you own rental property: copies of lease agreements plus certification of expenses such as mortgage loan payments, taxes, etc.

13. if you receive or pay alimony or child support: a copy of the divorce decree and deposit receipts or other proof

14. an estimate of the value of all your personal property: household goods, clothing, jewelry, hobby equipment, etc.

15. information about any bankruptcy or judgments

What to Expect from the 'Loan App'

Once you have assembled the vast bundle of necessary information, make an appointment to see the loan officer you have chosen. Because the application forms are complicated and confusing, loan officers prefer to fill out the form with the prospective borrower sitting close by. During the 'loan app,' the loan officer will discuss the various loan possibilities and will run calculations to see if you qualify for the size and type of loan you want. You will be given a written estimate of your closing costs and the monthly payment figures. The loan officer will then fill in the application form and will have you sign it. At the same time, you will also be asked to sign form letters to your employer and to the banks, credit unions or S&Ls where you have an account, requesting verification of employment and funds.

You must also leave a check for the cost of the credit report and appraisal (usually a total of $365 to $425). This is not refundable, even if the loan is not approved, and that is why loan officers take time to qualify you first. It should be noted that even if a loan officer's preliminary calculations indicate that you are qualified, the loan may be denied by the underwriters. Results of the credit report, the employment and financial verification, and the appraisal can darken an otherwise rosy picture.

Locking in the Rate

Sometime between now and closing, the interest you'll pay on your loan will be determined and "locked-in". Each lender has a different policy. Some automatically lock in the rate at the time of loan application. Others allow the rate to "float" until you lock in the rate, when you decide the interest rate that day is where you'd like it. Once the rate is locked, you'll be bound to that rate no matter what interest rates in general do, although some lenders offer an escape clause (at a price, of course). Rate locks have a time limit, often 30 to 60 days, so be sure to ask about your lender's policy.

A Timetable for Loan Processing

From here on, you are at the mercy of the loan officer, the U.S. Postal Service, the credit reporting agency, the appraiser, your bank and your employer. How quickly you receive your loan approval will depend upon the speed and efficiency of all of the above. Of course, applicants with out-of-state employers or bank accounts can expect a longer wait than those whose verification letters are mailed to local addresses. However, in general, the timetable for a typical new loan might go like this:

Day 1 Loan application
Days 2 - 7 Financial and employment verification letters sent by lender
Credit report and appraisal ordered by lender
Days 6 - 20 Appraiser inspects home (written appraisal sent to lender within one week)
Days 15 -30 Appraisal, credit report and completed verification letters received by lender

When all the documents have been received, the loan officer will examine the data and will put together a 'package' for the underwriters. A weak spot may have appeared that needs better explanation. For example, your credit report might show a current car loan, even though you paid it in full last month. Or perhaps your company's verification letter did not mention the $20,000 bonus you customarily earn. In these cases, the loan officer will ask you for additional documentation or proof, such as a letter from the automobile credit company, or a correction of the employment verification.

As soon as your loan officer has assembled a loan package that will present your strongest possible case, it is sent to the underwriters. Usually within 1 to 4 days, you will hear one of three answers: your loan has been approved, or your loan has been conditionally approved (approved only if you agree to accept certain conditions), or your loan has been denied. If your loan has not been approved, most lenders will allow the package to be resubmitted if new supporting information has been received. However, your application will have a much better chance of survival if all the weak spots are fortified before the underwriters find them.

Adequate Funds to Close

"Don't worry, I'll dig up the down payment somewhere," is a statement that guarantees a quick exit from any loan office. A borrower who cannot show sufficient funds for the down payment and closing costs will not get a loan. That sounds ridiculously elementary; of course you need to have enough money for closing. But has that money been sitting in your bank account since loan application? Or is it somewhere else at the moment? Your lender would like to know.

If your application clearly shows where the closing funds will be coming from, and if this amount is in cash or in an asset that is readily converted to cash (bonds, for instance), there will be no problem. But if your bank accounts do not show enough money to close and no other obvious assets are present, you will have to offer proof of sufficient funds before you will receive loan approval.

Gift Letters and Borrowed Down Payment

Perhaps a relative will be giving you money for the down payment. If so, the lender will want a 'gift letter' from the donor, stating clearly that this is a gift and repayment is not required. If, however, someone will be *lending* you the money, the loan officer will need to have some documentation of the loan, explaining just how and when the money is to be repaid. These private loan payments will be included in the qualifying calculations and may lower your borrowing limit. Lenders today often have restrictions on the amount of money that buyers receive from another source, whether from parents, the seller or a third party. Be sure to ask your loan officer what restrictions might apply.

Countdown to Closing

After your loan has been approved, your direct contact with the loan officer is over. The loan processing department prepares the documents that will be needed and sends them to the escrow company chosen to handle the closing. Even if you are simply refinancing your present home, there will still be an escrow closing.

In the following chapter, we'll estimate what your closing costs will be.

31

Loan Costs
& Escrow Closing

Financing a home can be an expensive proposition. Many borrowers are dumbfounded when they notice the bottom line of the closing cost estimate prepared by their loan officer. In today's financing, it is not at all unusual for a borrower to pay loan fees, closing costs and reserves of 7% or 8% of the loan amount. A buydown and discount points can push this total even higher. Add to this the down payment and you'll see why many buyers are priced out of the market before their application even gets to the underwriters for approval.

If you are buying a home, most of these fees must be paid in cash, either at the time of the loan application (the appraisal and credit check, for instance), or at closing. Sellers have closing costs, too, and these will be deducted from their proceeds at closing. Homeowners who are obtaining a refinance, equity loan or reverse annuity mortgage may be permitted to finance many of the closing costs right along with the loan, so cash may not be required. Nevertheless, it's wise to know what to expect right from the start, so you can plan your transaction wisely. If you realize, for example, that $5,000 or $6,000 of your cash reserves may have to be used for closing costs on a new loan, then you can make an informed decision about how to proceed.

CLOSING COSTS

	Conventional Loan	Conventional Refinance	FHA Loan	VA Loan	Assumption	Land Sales Contract	Estimated Loan Costs
BUYER'S USUAL COSTS							
Appraisal Fee	X	X	X	X	O		
Credit Report	X	X	X	X	X		
Loan Fee / Assumption Fee	X	X	X	X	X		
VA Funding Fee				X			
Discount Points	O	O	X	X			
Buydown Fee	O	O	O	O			
Mortgage Insurance Premium	O	O	X				
Underwriting Fee	X	X	X	X			
Document Preparation Fee	O	O	O	O			
Tax Service Fee	X	X	S	S			
Flood Hazard Report	X	X	X	X			
Survey Fee	O	O	O	O			
Re-inspection Fee	O	O	O	O			
Mortgagee's Title Insurance	X	X	X	X			
Excise Tax *	X		X	X	X	X	
Interest Payment	X	X	X	X	X		
Down Payment	X		X	O	X	X	
Homeowner's Insurance	X	X	X	X	X	X	
Tax Reserve	O	O	X	X	O	O	
COSTS: BUYERS and/or SELLERS							
Tax Prorates	X	X	X	X	X	X	
Escrow Fee	X	X	X	S	X	X	
Recording Fees	X	X	X	X	X	X	
Sales Tax *	X	X	X	X	X	X	
Transfer Tax **	X		X	X	X	X	
SELLER'S USUAL COSTS							
Owner's Title Insurance Policy	X	X	X	X	X	X	
Reconveyance Fee	X	X	X	X			
Real Estate Commission	X		X	X	X	X	

√ (marks at Tax Service Fee and Escrow Fee rows)

* Washington State only   ** Washington County only
X - fee usually charged   O - fee sometimes charged
S - seller pays entire fee

This chart shows the types of fees customarily charged for different methods of financing. The blank spaces to the right of the chart are for your personal use, to be filled with your own estimated costs. Later in this chapter you'll find a description of each fee, plus information to help you determine what you'll be charged. Of course, when you do apply for a loan, your loan officer will supply a detailed estimate of your closing costs. This chart simply offers an overall view of financing expenses, to let you know in advance what to expect.

Who Pays What? And How Much?

When it comes to divvying up the closing costs between buyer and seller, the usual practice is for buyers to pay for any costs related to the new loan, and any fees or reserves required by the lender. Some of the buyers' costs may be paid for by the sellers (according to the lender's policy), but this should be negotiated at the time the offer is made to purchase the home. Occasionally, these days, buyers work with a real estate agent or broker who represents them, rather than the seller (a buyer's broker). In that case, the commission would be paid by the buyers.

Sellers customarily pay any fees necessary to pay off the existing loan and record the satisfaction of debt. If the home was listed and sold by a real estate firm, the seller will pay the commission. Escrow fees are usually split between buyer and seller unless the buyer is securing a VA loan (then seller pays the full fee). The seller will usually provide title insurance for the buyer, and the buyer will pick up the tab on the lender's policy. Property taxes that have been paid (or not yet paid) will have to be sorted out at closing (see Tax Pro-rates in the list that follows) and will end up being a cost to one of the parties. Here is an explanation of the items found on the chart. Many have names that are thoroughly mystifying to even seasoned borrowers.

Buyer's Usual Costs:

Appraisal Fee: This fee is paid at time of loan application, to cover the cost of appraising the home. Estimate $350 (conventional) for a single-family home, but the figure varies. It can be higher for appraisals in out-of-the-way areas where mileage expenses will be added, or for more complex appraisals. (FHA appraisals: estimate $300 for most single-family homes; on VA loans: estimate $325 for single-family, plus mileage, if necessary.)

Credit Report: Paid at the time of loan application, a credit report on the borrower can cost from $65 to $75, plus an additional charge if it's necessary to "clean up" and recheck certain items.

Loan Fee: Also known as the Loan Origination Fee, it is a fee charged by the lender to cover the basic cost of making the loan. It is usually expressed as a percentage of the loan amount. Conventional loan fees today vary from about 1% to 2% (more if discount points are included in the figure). FHA & VA Loan Origination Fees: 1%. On assumptions, expect an Assumption Fee.

VA Funding Fee: Charged in addition to the 1% loan origination fee, this fee supports the loan guaranty program. For VA loans with less than a 5% down payment: 1.875% of the loan amount. With a 5% to 9.99% down payment: 1.375% of the loan amount; with a 10% or greater down payment: a 1.125% fee is charged.

Discount Points: These have been discussed in the chapter on Loans with Buydowns, as well as in the FHA and VA chapters. One discount point equals one percent of the loan amount. Not present on all loans.

Buydown Fee: The interest rate may be lowered through the use of a buydown. Fees vary considerably. For more information, see the chapter on Loans with Buydowns.

Mortgage Insurance Premium: Varies with type and amount of loan. Refer to Part II, Conventional Loans and also the chapter on FHA loans for information on how to estimate the premium. Note that on monthly premiums, an extra month's premium may be collected at closing if the first payment will not be due immediately.

Underwriting Fee and Document Preparation Fee: These are simply service fees ("junk fees", as insiders call them) added by lenders to cover miscellaneous paperwork preparation. Some lenders charge one of the two, but not the second. Other lenders charge both. Allow a total of $200 to $300.

Tax Service Fee: The fee to provide the lender with an accurate report of the property tax status (delinquent, paid in full, etc.). The seller must pay this on all FHA and VA loans. Estimate $57 to $67.

Flood Hazard Report: Another lender requirement, this one is mercifully inexpensive (estimate $5 to $25), but it can lead to extra expense in another category. It's a report to determine whether or not the home's in a 100-year flood plain. If it is, most lenders require a rider to the homeowner's policy, providing flood protection.

Survey Fee: For new construction and most loans over $100,000 the lenders and/or title insurance companies require foundation surveys. Estimate $200.

Re-inspection Fee: If repairs are required by the FHA or VA appraiser, the property must be re-inspected. Cost: $45 on FHA or VA, $75 on conventional loans. The first re-inspection is usually paid for by the seller, subsequent re-inspections are often paid for by the buyer.

Mortgagee's Title Insurance: Most lenders require buyers (or owners refinancing) to pay for what is known as a Mortgagee's ALTA policy. The value of the policy will

219

be based on the loan amount. See a sample rate table in Appendix III. In both states, additional endorsements are usually added to the basic policy: protection for the lender in matters of environmental liens, CCR violations, and even errors in the street address. These add around $35 to the mortgagee's premium in Oregon, but are usually included in the basic premium in Washington. For ARM loans, there's an ARM endorsement to be added; estimate $50 in Oregon, usually no additional charge in Washington.

Excise Tax: Oregonians, you're off the hook on this one. Washingtonians pay a basic state excise rate that's currently 1.53% of the sales price, plus additional for individual counties. Your escrow officer or LPO can give you the current figure for your locale.

Interest Payment: Although interest is paid at the end of each month, the first monthly payment may not be scheduled to start for 45 days or so after closing. Therefore, the first interest payment will be collected at closing, based on the number of days before the payments start.

Down Payment: While not actually a closing cost, it is a cash payment that is collected at or before closing.

Homeowner's Insurance: One year to 14 months of insurance must be paid at closing. The policy value must be equal to or greater than the loan amount.

Tax Reserves: Property tax reserves are required on most government loans and on most conventional loans over 80% LTV. No matter whether you live in Oregon or Washington, reserves are calculated so that by the time the next tax bill comes due (in Oregon, November 15th and in Washington, April 30th and October 31st, your reserve account will be brimming with sufficient funds to pay the bill in full. As an example, a closing that takes place on August 15th in Oregon will require 10 months of reserves. (The September and October payments will each include a remaining month to make up the full year's worth.)

In Washington, property taxes may be paid in full on April 30th, but more frequently are paid in half-payments twice a year, even by lenders. A reserve account must contain usually only one-half the year's total tax amount by the due date. Therefore a closing on August 15th in Washington will require only 5 1/2 months of reserves.

With any of the costs that are based upon the closing date, the lender may require an extra month's payment (or even two) at closing if the first scheduled monthly loan payment will not begin for several weeks. This can certainly affect your cash reserves so be sure to ask both your loan officer and escrow officer (or LPO) what will be required.

Costs for Buyers and/or Sellers:

Tax Pro-Rates: In almost every transaction one party (the buyer or the seller) must reimburse the other for property taxes paid or owed. Oregon and Washington have different tax payment schedules and so pro-rates are handled differently in each state. In Oregon, the tax bill is due each year on November 15th. This bill covers the one-year period from the previous July 1st to the following June 30th. If the seller pays the bill in full in November but sells the home two months later, on January 15th, the buyer will owe the seller five and one-half months worth of taxes, since they have been paid through June 30th of that year. If the closing were to take place on August 15th, the seller would be responsible for the taxes up to that date. Since the new tax bill will not be printed until November, there is no way for the seller to pay the county directly for the period from July 1st through August 15th. The county will not accept funds until the bill has been established. Therefore, the seller will reimburse the buyer at closing for one and one-half months

221

of taxes, based on the previous year's rate; the buyer will then pay the bill in full when it comes due, even if the bill turns out to be higher than the estimated reimbursement.

In Washington, the April 30th tax bill officially covers the period from January 1st through December 30th of that same year, although most homeowners opt to pay one-half of the bill by April 30th (to cover the period through June 30th), and the balance on October 31st (to pay for the tax period from July 1st through December 31st.) Therefore at a closing on August 15th (before the October bill has arrived or been paid), the seller would owe the buyer one and one-half months worth of tax, assuming the seller had paid one half of the total tax in April. For a closing on November 15th, the buyer would reimburse the seller for one and one-half months worth of tax.

Buyers: *Here's an easy, if less exact, way to estimate your total property tax reserves plus pro-rates. In Oregon, estimate 12 months (one full year) of property tax due at closing; in Washington, estimate 6 months worth of property tax due at closing to cover both reserves and prorates.*

Escrow Fee: The fee charged by the escrow company for the services of the escrow officer in preparing the closing documents and conducting the escrow closing. Varies with sales price (or loan amount for a refinance) and differs from company to company. Fee is split between buyer and seller except for VA loans where the seller pays the entire fee. (In Spokane County, closings are handled by attorneys or limited practice officers [LPOs]. Estimate a total fee of approximately 1/2 of 1% of the sales price, split between buyer and seller.) Escrow fees in Washington are typically much higher than those in Oregon. You'll find sample escrow rates in Appendix II. Many escrow companies offer a reduction for refinance closings (count on 25% discount). There is often a slightly lower fee on new construction.

Recording Fees: The cost for recording the deed and the loan documents varies slightly from county to county and is based upon the number of pages recorded. Estimate $25 to $45 for a conventional fixed-rate loan or not-too-lengthy land sales contract, slightly higher for government financing or a more complicated loan, such as an ARM.

Sales Tax: Again, for Washington only, sales tax is due on the escrow fee and title insurance premium.

Transfer Tax: For property in Washington County, Oregon only. Tax is $.50 per $1,000 for both buyer and seller. Not charged for refinances.

Seller's Usual Costs:

Owner's Title Insurance Policy: Premium paid by the seller to provide insurance for the purchaser against possible defects of title. See table of costs in Appendix III.

Reconveyance Fee: When an existing loan is paid off, a reconveyance fee will be charged by the lender. Sellers: estimate approximately $35 to $50. (On refinances, the the owner pays.)

Real Estate Commission: In most transactions, paid by the seller at closing. Where the agent legally represents the buyer rather than the seller, the commission is paid by the buyer.

The Escrow Closing

In Oregon the closing is customarily held at the office of a title insurance company. Washington, with its higher escrow rates, has provided a more fertile ground for the growth of escrow companies, and closings are often held at such firms. Closings in Washington may also take place at the escrow office of a title insurance company or, in some parts of the state, at the mortgage lender's own

223

escrow department. In Spokane County, closings take place at an attorney's office, in the presence of an attorney or an LPO, a limited practice officer.

No matter where the closing takes place, the procedure is very much the same whether you are buying, selling or refinancing your present home. The closing is conducted by an escrow officer, LPO or attorney, the person responsible for assembling the necessary documents, calculating the buyers' and sellers' cost sheets, carrying out the lender's instructions, recording the deed and loan documents, and disbursing the proceeds.

By law, escrow officers must remain neutral; they may not side with one party over another. Their job is to handle the paperwork and funds in an impartial manner. To preserve this neutrality they must follow only written instructions that have been signed by both parties or by the lender and borrower. If a buyer calls to say, "I want you to hold back $50 until the seller repairs a crack in the ceiling," the escrow agent is powerless to comply, unless the request is presented in writing and agreed to by the seller as well. An escrow officer may not attempt to negotiate a sticky point in a transaction; that is what real estate agents are able to do. For serious difficulties, ask your attorney to smooth the path.

Closing Procedure in the Pacific Northwest

Closings here are less formal than in many eastern states where buyers, sellers and their attorneys face each other across a formidable conference table. In the Pacific Northwest, escrow closings are usually private affairs. When closing day arrives, buyers and sellers make separate appointments with the escrow officer. Each party meets at a different time, to review and sign the documents and, in the case of the buyer, to bring in a certified check for the down payment and closing costs. (The escrow officer will advise the buyer of the required amount a day or two in advance.) When both parties have signed, the escrow officer will send the loan documents to the lender for a last-minute check. Once the lender approves, the trust deed (or mortgage) will be delivered to the county courthouse to be recorded. The lender will issue a check to fund the loan and will send it to the escrow officer. Finally the warranty deed, signed by the seller, giving title to the buyer, will be recorded.

Do You Need the Services of an Attorney?

Should an attorney advise you or represent you at closing? In eastern and midwestern states, where title insurance is not frequently used, the answer to this question would be a definite "yes." There, attorneys are needed to do a title search of the property, assuring the buyer that the title is good and marketable. A friend of mine who owns a home in Ohio discovered to her dismay that someone else owned her entire front yard and wanted an exorbitant price for it. She had bought the home without a title search.

Here, in the Pacific Northwest, the use of title insurance is customary. The seller provides it for the buyer and the borrower buys a policy for the lender, to protect against unforeseen defects of title. The title insurance company conducts a title search and issues a preliminary report to both buyers and sellers. When you receive your copy, read it thoroughly. Any surprise encumbrances should be called to the attention of your real estate agent, escrow officer or attorney before closing. For example, the preliminary report may show a lien against the property that neither the buyer nor seller knew about. Unless the lien can be removed, it must be paid off at closing, the closing must be postponed until the problem can be resolved, or the buyer must agree to allow that lien to remain. If, as in the case of my friend, you later discover that a stranger owns your yard, the title insurance company may use the necessary legal means to correct the situation, unless, of course, you were advised in the preliminary report that you were not purchasing that part of the property.

With title insurance, an attorney is not absolutely essential for a simple transaction. Most buyers and sellers in Washington and Oregon do not consult an attorney for the purchase, sale or refinancing of a home, except in Spokane County where attorneys routinely handle closings. There are times, however, when it's very, very prudent to have an attorney prepare legal documents or review paperwork before you sign. Here are some guidelines to help you recognize the danger zone.

Seek Legal Advice...

- If you're confused about *any* document you're asked to sign, at any stage in the homebuying process, seek legal advice before you sign.

- If you're entering into a seller-financing agreement of any type, it's wise to have your attorney draft the documents or review your documents before you sign.

- If you are entering into a 'sweat equity' agreement, where the buyer will be making repairs to the home as all or part of the down payment, ask your attorney to draw up an agreement to cover all aspects of the work, to protect your rights, whether you're the buyer or seller.

- If you are considering a shared appreciation or equity participation transaction, consult an attorney before proceeding.

- If, for any reason, you are not protected by title insurance, have an attorney check the title to see that it is clear.

In general, if you have any doubts at all, or if your transaction is a complicated one, be sure to seek legal advice. Real estate mistakes can end up costing more than the property itself. If nothing else, professional advice is a pretty inexpensive price to pay for peace of mind.

Disbursement of Funds

The proceeds from the closing will be disbursed by the escrow officer, LPO or attorney after the documents have been recorded. Because the post-signing activities take time, sellers should expect a wait of one to several days before receiving a check. Lenders often want 24 to 48 hours to review the signed loan papers, and there may be a day's delay in transmitting the papers to the county for recording. Discuss the timing with your escrow officer in advance so that you will know what to expect.

32

A Final Word

N o one said financing a home would be *easy*. Nobody promised *fun*. (At least, I certainly didn't.) But on the other hand, getting a loan doesn't have to be the anguishing, high-stress, white-knuckle trauma it often turns out to be.

You can change that. You can very easily tilt the odds in your favor. True, you don't have control over the rise and fall of interest rates. You can't wish a higher LTV or easier qualifying ratios and make them come true. But you can approach financing with the self-confidence that comes from knowing exactly where you stand. It involves a certain amount of reading, research, evaluation and calculation, but after finishing this book, you're well on your way. Now the next step is a real-life test run—combining the basic knowledge you've acquired with actual market information and current interest rates.

I think you'll find it's not too difficult (and maybe even almost fun) now that you've had a head start comparison shopping at home. I wish you great success in your search for the perfect financing!

APPENDIX

APPENDIX I

Loan Amortization Schedule

Use this chart to determine what your monthly principal and interest payment will be. Real estate loan payments are amortized over the term of the loan. That is, the payments are calculated to include the correct amount of principal and interest so that the loan balance will be zero at the end of the term.

Step 1: Find the applicable interest rate in the top row.

Step 2: Find the term of the loan in the column on the left.

Step 3: Trace down the rate column and across the term row to the square where the two meet. Remember this factor.

Step 4: Move the decimal point in your loan amount three places to the left.

Example: $57,850. becomes 57.850.

Step 5: Multiply this number by the factor you have found on the chart.

Example: A 10% loan with a term of 30 years would have a factor of 8.78 according to the chart. If the loan balance is $57,850, we would multiply 57.850 by 8.78 and find that our monthly payment (principal and interest) would be $507.92.

%	4.00	4.25	4.50	4.75	5.00	5.25	5.50	5.75	6.00	6.25	6.50	6.75	7.00	7.25	%
1	85.15	85.26	85.38	85.49	85.61	85.72	85.84	85.95	86.07	86.18	86.30	86.41	86.53	86.64	1
	43.42	43.54	43.65	43.76	43.87	43.98	44.10	44.21	44.32	44.43	44.55	44.66	44.77	44.89	
	29.52	29.64	29.75	29.86	29.97	30.08	30.20	30.31	30.42	30.54	30.65	30.76	30.88	30.99	
	22.58	22.69	22.80	22.92	23.03	23.14	23.26	23.37	23.49	23.60	23.71	23.83	23.95	24.06	
5	18.42	18.53	18.64	18.76	18.87	18.99	19.10	19.22	19.33	19.45	19.57	19.68	19.80	19.92	5
	15.65	15.76	15.87	15.99	16.10	16.22	16.34	16.46	16.57	16.69	16.81	16.93	17.05	17.17	
	13.67	13.78	13.90	14.02	14.13	14.25	14.37	14.49	14.61	14.73	14.85	14.97	15.09	15.22	
	12.19	12.31	12.42	12.54	12.66	12.78	12.90	13.02	13.14	13.26	13.39	13.51	13.63	13.76	
	11.04	11.16	11.28	11.40	11.52	11.64	11.76	11.88	12.01	12.13	12.25	12.38	12.51	12.63	
10	10.12	10.24	10.36	10.48	10.61	10.73	10.85	10.98	11.10	11.23	11.35	11.48	11.61	11.74	10
	9.38	9.50	9.62	9.74	9.86	9.99	10.11	10.24	10.37	10.49	10.62	10.75	10.88	11.02	
	8.76	8.88	9.00	9.12	9.25	9.37	9.50	9.63	9.76	9.89	10.02	10.15	10.28	10.42	
	8.23	8.35	8.48	8.60	8.73	8.86	8.99	9.12	9.25	9.38	9.51	9.65	9.78	9.92	
	7.78	7.92	8.03	8.16	8.29	8.42	8.55	8.68	8.81	8.95	9.08	9.22	9.35	9.49	
15	7.40	7.52	7.65	7.78	7.91	8.04	8.17	8.30	8.44	8.57	8.71	8.85	8.99	9.13	15
	7.06	7.19	7.32	7.45	7.58	7.71	7.84	7.98	8.11	8.25	8.39	8.53	8.67	8.81	
	6.76	6.89	7.02	7.15	7.29	7.42	7.56	7.69	7.83	7.97	8.11	8.25	8.40	8.54	
	6.50	6.63	6.76	6.90	7.03	7.17	7.30	7.44	7.58	7.72	7.87	8.01	8.16	8.30	
	6.27	6.40	6.53	6.67	6.80	6.94	7.08	7.22	7.36	7.50	7.65	7.79	7.94	8.09	
20	6.06	6.19	6.33	6.46	6.60	6.74	6.88	7.02	7.16	7.31	7.46	7.60	7.75	7.90	20
	5.87	6.01	6.14	6.28	6.42	6.56	6.70	6.84	6.99	7.14	7.28	7.43	7.58	7.74	
	5.70	5.84	5.97	6.11	6.25	6.39	6.54	6.68	6.83	6.98	7.13	7.28	7.43	7.59	
	5.55	5.68	5.82	5.96	6.10	6.25	6.39	6.54	6.69	6.84	6.99	7.14	7.30	7.46	
	5.41	5.54	5.68	5.83	5.97	6.11	6.26	6.41	6.56	6.71	6.87	7.02	7.18	7.34	
25	5.28	5.42	5.56	5.70	5.85	5.99	6.14	6.29	6.44	6.60	6.75	6.91	7.07	7.23	25
	5.16	5.30	5.44	5.59	5.73	5.88	6.03	6.18	6.33	6.49	6.65	6.81	6.97	7.13	
	5.05	5.19	5.34	5.48	5.63	5.78	5.93	6.08	6.24	6.40	6.56	6.72	6.88	7.04	
	4.95	5.09	5.24	5.39	5.54	5.69	5.84	5.99	6.15	6.31	6.47	6.63	6.80	6.96	
	4.86	5.00	5.15	5.30	5.45	5.60	5.76	5.91	6.07	6.23	6.39	6.56	6.72	6.89	
30	4.77	4.92	5.07	5.22	5.37	5.52	5.68	5.84	6.00	6.16	6.32	6.49	6.65	6.82	30

Appendix I: Loan Amortization Schedule

Year	7.50	7.75	8.00	8.25	8.50	8.75	9.00	9.25	9.50	9.75	10.00	10.25	10.50	10.75
1	86.76	86.87	86.99	87.10	87.22	87.34	87.45	87.57	87.68	87.80	87.92	88.03	88.15	88.27
2	45.00	45.11	45.23	45.34	45.46	45.57	45.68	45.80	45.91	46.03	46.14	46.26	46.38	46.49
3	31.11	31.22	31.34	31.45	31.57	31.68	31.80	31.92	32.03	32.15	32.27	32.38	32.50	32.62
4	24.18	24.30	24.41	24.53	24.65	24.77	24.89	25.00	25.12	25.24	25.36	25.48	25.60	25.72
5	20.04	20.16	20.28	20.40	20.52	20.64	20.76	20.88	21.00	21.12	21.25	21.37	21.49	21.62
6	17.29	17.41	17.53	17.66	17.78	17.90	18.03	18.15	18.27	18.40	18.53	18.65	18.78	18.91
7	15.34	15.46	15.59	15.71	15.84	15.96	16.09	16.22	16.34	16.47	16.60	16.73	16.86	16.99
8	13.88	14.01	14.14	14.26	14.39	14.52	14.65	14.78	14.91	15.04	15.17	15.31	15.44	15.57
9	12.76	12.89	13.02	13.15	13.28	13.41	13.54	13.68	13.81	13.94	14.08	14.21	14.35	14.49
10	11.87	12.00	12.13	12.27	12.40	12.53	12.67	12.80	12.94	13.08	13.22	13.35	13.49	13.63
11	11.15	11.28	11.42	11.55	11.69	11.82	11.96	12.10	12.24	12.38	12.52	12.66	12.80	12.95
12	10.55	10.69	10.82	10.96	11.10	11.24	11.38	11.52	11.66	11.81	11.95	12.10	12.24	12.39
13	10.05	10.19	10.33	10.47	10.61	10.75	10.90	11.04	11.19	11.33	11.48	11.63	11.78	11.92
14	9.63	9.77	9.91	10.06	10.20	10.34	10.49	10.64	10.78	10.93	11.08	11.23	11.38	11.54
15	9.27	9.41	9.56	9.70	9.85	9.99	10.14	10.29	10.44	10.59	10.75	10.90	11.05	11.21
16	8.96	9.10	9.25	9.40	9.54	9.69	9.85	10.00	10.15	10.30	10.46	10.62	10.77	10.93
17	8.69	8.83	8.98	9.13	9.28	9.43	9.59	9.74	9.90	10.05	10.21	10.37	10.53	10.69
18	8.45	8.60	8.75	8.90	9.05	9.21	9.36	9.52	9.68	9.84	10.00	10.16	10.32	10.49
19	8.24	8.39	8.55	8.70	8.85	9.01	9.17	9.33	9.49	9.65	9.81	9.98	10.14	10.31
20	8.06	8.21	8.36	8.52	8.68	8.84	9.00	9.16	9.32	9.49	9.65	9.82	9.98	10.15
21	7.89	8.05	8.20	8.36	8.52	8.68	8.85	9.01	9.17	9.34	9.51	9.68	9.85	10.02
22	7.75	7.90	8.06	8.22	8.38	8.55	8.71	8.88	9.04	9.21	9.38	9.55	9.73	9.90
23	7.61	7.77	7.93	8.10	8.26	8.43	8.59	8.76	8.93	9.10	9.27	9.44	9.62	9.79
24	7.50	7.66	7.82	7.98	8.15	8.32	8.49	8.66	8.83	9.00	9.17	9.35	9.52	9.70
25	7.39	7.55	7.72	7.88	8.05	8.22	8.39	8.56	8.74	8.91	9.09	9.26	9.44	9.62
26	7.29	7.46	7.63	7.79	7.96	8.13	8.31	8.48	8.66	8.83	9.01	9.19	9.37	9.55
27	7.21	7.37	7.54	7.71	7.88	8.06	8.23	8.41	8.58	8.76	8.94	9.12	9.30	9.49
28	7.13	7.30	7.47	7.64	7.81	7.99	8.16	8.34	8.52	8.70	8.88	9.06	9.25	9.43
29	7.06	7.23	7.40	7.57	7.75	7.92	8.10	8.28	8.46	8.64	8.82	9.01	9.19	9.38
30	6.99	7.16	7.34	7.51	7.69	7.87	8.05	8.23	8.41	8.59	8.78	8.96	9.15	9.33

YEAR

Year	11.00	11.25	11.50	11.75	12.00	12.25	12.50	12.75	13.00	13.25	13.50	13.75	14.00	14.25
1	88.38	88.50	88.62	88.73	88.85	88.97	89.08	89.20	89.32	89.43	89.55	89.67	89.79	89.90
2	46.61	46.72	46.84	46.96	47.07	47.19	47.31	47.42	47.54	47.66	47.78	47.89	48.01	48.13
3	32.74	32.86	32.98	33.10	33.21	33.33	33.45	33.57	33.69	33.81	33.94	34.06	34.18	34.30
4	25.85	25.97	26.09	26.21	26.33	26.46	26.58	26.70	26.83	26.95	27.08	27.20	27.33	27.45
5	21.74	21.87	21.99	22.12	22.24	22.37	22.50	22.63	22.75	22.88	23.01	23.14	23.27	23.40
6	19.03	19.16	19.29	19.42	19.55	19.68	19.81	19.94	20.07	20.21	20.34	20.47	20.61	20.74
7	17.12	17.25	17.39	17.52	17.65	17.79	17.92	18.06	18.19	18.33	18.46	18.60	18.74	18.88
8	15.71	15.84	15.98	16.12	16.25	16.39	16.53	16.67	16.81	16.95	17.09	17.23	17.37	17.51
9	14.63	14.76	14.90	15.04	15.18	15.33	15.47	15.61	15.75	15.90	16.04	16.19	16.33	16.48
10	13.78	13.92	14.06	14.20	14.35	14.49	14.64	14.78	14.93	15.08	15.23	15.38	15.53	15.68
11	13.09	13.24	13.38	13.53	13.68	13.83	13.98	14.13	14.28	14.43	14.58	14.73	14.89	15.04
12	12.54	12.68	12.83	12.98	13.13	13.29	13.44	13.59	13.75	13.90	14.06	14.21	14.37	14.53
13	12.08	12.23	12.38	12.53	12.69	12.84	13.00	13.15	13.31	13.47	13.63	13.79	13.95	14.11
14	11.69	11.85	12.00	12.16	12.31	12.47	12.63	12.79	12.95	13.11	13.28	13.44	13.60	13.77
15	11.37	11.52	11.68	11.84	12.00	12.16	12.33	12.49	12.65	12.82	12.98	13.15	13.32	13.49
16	11.09	11.25	11.41	11.57	11.74	11.90	12.07	12.23	12.40	12.57	12.74	12.91	13.08	13.25
17	10.85	11.02	11.18	11.35	11.51	11.68	11.85	12.02	12.19	12.36	12.53	12.70	12.87	13.05
18	10.65	10.82	10.98	11.15	11.32	11.49	11.66	11.83	12.00	12.18	12.35	12.53	12.70	12.88
19	10.47	10.64	10.81	10.98	11.15	11.33	11.50	11.67	11.85	12.03	12.20	12.38	12.56	12.74
20	10.32	10.49	10.66	10.84	11.01	11.19	11.36	11.54	11.72	11.89	12.07	12.25	12.44	12.62
21	10.19	10.36	10.54	10.71	10.89	11.06	11.24	11.42	11.60	11.78	11.96	12.15	12.33	12.51
22	10.07	10.25	10.42	10.60	10.78	10.96	11.14	11.32	11.50	11.69	11.87	12.05	12.24	12.43
23	9.97	10.15	10.33	10.51	10.69	10.87	11.05	11.23	11.42	11.60	11.79	11.97	12.16	12.35
24	9.88	10.06	10.24	10.42	10.60	10.79	10.97	11.16	11.34	11.53	11.72	11.91	12.10	12.29
25	9.80	9.98	10.16	10.35	10.53	10.72	10.90	11.09	11.28	11.47	11.66	11.85	12.04	12.23
26	9.73	9.91	10.10	10.28	10.47	10.66	10.84	11.03	11.22	11.41	11.60	11.80	11.99	12.18
27	9.67	9.85	10.04	10.23	10.41	10.60	10.79	10.98	11.17	11.37	11.56	11.75	11.95	12.14
28	9.61	9.80	9.99	10.18	10.37	10.56	10.75	10.94	11.13	11.32	11.52	11.71	11.91	12.10
29	9.57	9.75	9.94	10.13	10.32	10.52	10.71	10.90	11.09	11.29	11.48	11.68	11.88	12.07
30	9.52	9.71	9.90	10.09	10.29	10.48	10.67	10.87	11.06	11.26	11.45	11.65	11.85	12.05

YEAR

APPENDIX II

Sample Escrow Rates*

Sales Price:	For Oregon:	For Washington:
$50,000	$290	$400
$75,000	$315	$450
$100,000	$340	$500
$125,000	$365	$525
$150,000	$390	$550
$175,000	$415	$575
$200,000	$440	$600
$250,000	$490	$650
$300,000	$540	$700

*These rates are an average of escrow rates charged by companies in each state. They are intended to give you an approximate estimate of the costs you will encounter, however rate schedules vary widely, especially in Washington. You'll find some escrow rates considerably lower that those listed, while others are much higher. Remember that the fee will be split between buyer and seller, except with VA loans (seller pays all) and refinances, of course (deduct 25%).

APPENDIX III

Sample Title Insurance Rates

Policy Value:	Owner's Policy:	Mortgagee's Policy:
$ 40,000	$285	$150
$ 60,000	$360	$160
$ 80,000	$420	$180
$100,000	$480	$200
$120,000	$520	$210
$140,000	$560	$220
$160,000	$600	$235
$180,000	$640	$250
$200,000	$680	$260
$250,000	$780	$290
$300,000	$880	$320
$350,000	$990	$350

The value of the Owner's Policy is the sales price; the value of the Mortgagee's Policy is the loan amount.

235

APPENDIX IV
FHA Mortgage Insurance Premiums

The following tables show the percentages used to calculate Mortgage Insurance Premiums (UFMIPs and MIPs) on most types types of FHA loans:

Upfront and Annual MIP Premiums for Loans with Terms Greater Than 15 Years			
Upfront	LTV Ratio	Premium	Years
3.00	89.99 & Under	.50	7
3.00	90.00 - 95.00	.50	12
3.00	95.01 & Over	.50	30

Upfront and Annual MIP Premiums for Loans with Terms 15 Years or Less			
Upfront	LTV Ratio	Premium	Years
2.00	89.99 & Under	None	n/a
2.00	90.00 - 95.00	.25	4
2.00	95.01 & Over	.25	8

INDEX